Table of Contents

Do we count fathers in Minnesota?

Searching for key indicators of the well-being of fathers & families

List of tables and figures.. 2

Executive summary.. 4

Preface.. 6

Introduction.. 7

Section 1: Searching for Data:
Research statistics about fathers..11

CH. 1: Well-being of Minnesota's children: context for studying well-being of fathers........ 13

CH. 2: Defining fatherhood... 14

CH. 3: Demographic profile of Minnesota's fathers.................................. 18

CH. 4: Family structure 21

CH. 5: Economic indicators.. 29

CH. 6: Barriers to father involvement.. 36

CH. 7: Special populations of Minnesota's fathers................................... 43

CH. 8: Fathers' physical health and mental health................................... 47

Section 2: Filling the gaps:
Surveys to broaden our base of understanding.................................. 49

CH. 9: Father-child involvement.. 51

CH. 10: Services and programs for Minnesota's fathers.......................... 64

Section 3: Final words.. 67

CH. 11: Initial recommendations... 69

CH. 12: Bibliography and Acknowledgements... 73

List of tables and figures

Chapter 1   **The Well-Being of Minnesota's Children**
Table 1.1   Measure of the condition of children in Minnesota
Table 1.2   Rank of Minnesota's neighboring states on measures of child well-being

Chapter 2   **Defining Fatherhood**
Table 2.1   Identifying fathers for newborns: Minnesota's birth statistics

Chapter 3   **Demographic Profile of Minnesota's Fathers**
Figure 3.1   Father's age at the birth of first child
Figure 3.2   Number of biological children fathered by U.S. men
Figure 3.3   Race / ethnicity of Minnesota's birth fathers
Figure 3.4   Educational attainment of Minnesota's birth fathers
Figure 3.5   Educational attainment of Minnesota's fathers
Figure 3.6   Fertility: Number of biological children, per man

Chapter 4   **Family Structure**
Figure 4.1   Percent of parents currently married
Figure 4.2   Family groups with children under 18
Figure 4.3   Marriages and divorces
Table 4.1   Statewide percentages of marriages and divorces
Figure 4.4   Living arrangements of Minnesota's children under 18 years
Table 4.2   Married-couple families
Table 4.3   Male-headed families
Figure 4.5   Prevalence of multiple-partner fertility among men increases with age
Figure 4.6   Marital status of Minnesota males 15 years and over
Figure 4.7   Family composition, living arrangements of Minnesota's students
Figure 4.8   National employment status of custodial parents
Figure 4.9   National poverty rates of custodial parents
Figure 4.10   Children living with their single fathers
Figure 4.11   Father closeness and adolescent drug abuse: The impact of family structure
Figure 4.12   Minnesota household projections
Figure 4.13   Minnesota projected change in type of households

Chapter 5   **Economic Indicators**
Table 5.1   Employment status: Percent of both parents or single parent in the labor force
Figure 5.1   Family income and earnings
Table 5.2   Minnesota parental education and economic security
Figure 5.2   Rental housing: Percent of families renting their homes
Figure 5.3   Minnesota child support collections by source
Figure 5.4   Percent of custodial parents awarded child support
Figure 5.5   Custodial parents receiving part or full child support payments due
Table 5.3   Stay-at-home fathers
Figure 5.6   Fathers' health care coverage
Figure 5.7   Minnesota male-headed families: Health care coverage
Figure 5.8   Income of male householder families in Minnesota
Figure 5.9   Employment of male householder families in Minnesota
Figure 5.10   Men receiving welfare
Table 5.4   Income adequacy in Minnesota

Chapter 6   **Barriers to Father Involvement**
Figure 6.1   Minnesota Department of Corrections adult inmate population

List of tables and figures

Table 6.1	Children and families of military personnel
Figure 6.2	Perpetrators of child maltreatment
Figure 6.3	Child welfare cases: Parent involvement in case planning, mothers vs. fathers
Figure 6.4	Child welfare cases: Parent involvement in case planning, Minnesota vs. U.S.
Figure 6.5	Frequency of parent / child visits for families engaged in child welfare cases
Figure 6.6	Child welfare cases: Efforts made to maintain the parent / child relationship
Figure 6.7	Identifying nonresident fathers
Figure 6.8	Children with no biological father in their home who have never seen their father
Chapter 7	**Special Populations of Minnesota's Fathers**
Table 7.1	Fathers' statistics: Fathers of teen mothers' firstborn children
Figure 7.1	Teen mothers' marriage status and living arrangements
Figure 7.2	Father of firstborn child to teen mother: Father's contact with child
Figure 7.3	Birth rates for teenagers 15-19 years
Table 7.2	Grandparents in Minnesota
Table 7.3	Same-sex male partner households
Chapter 8	**Fathers' Physical Health and Mental Health**
Figure 8.1	Health status of fathers
Figure 8.2	Mental health status of fathers
Figure 8.3	Suicide rate per 100,000
Chapter 9	**Father-Child Involvement**
Table 9.1	Rating of fatherhood role activities
Table 9.2	Father activities with children ages 0-4
Table 9.3	Father activities with children 5-12
Table 9.4	Fathers' satisfaction with parenting
Table 9.5	Fathers' self-rating of fathering quality
Figure 9.1	Best parts of parenting for fathers
Figure 9.2	Most challenging parts of fatherhood
Figure 9.3	Sources of social support for fathers
Table 9.6	Ages of fathers who responded to survey
Table 9.7	Race / ethnicity of fathers in survey versus Minnesota
Table 9.8	Education levels of fathers in survey versus Minnesota
Table 9.9	Marital status of fathers in survey versus Minnesota
Table 9.10	Community type of fathers: Survey respondents versus Minnesota
Figure 9.4	Children represented in the survey: Ages of eldest children 0-4
Figure 9.5	Children represented in the survey: Ages of eldest children 5-12
Figure 9.6	Activities with children younger than 5 years old: Based on fathers' education
Figure 9.7	Activities with children younger than 5 years old: Based on fathers' residence
Figure 9.8	How dads define fatherhood
Figure 9.9	Parental communication: Father vs. mother
Chapter 10	**Services and Programs for Minnesota's Fathers**
Figure 10.1	Minnesota's regional fatherhood service providers
Figure 10.2	Number of agencies providing each type of service to Minnesota's fathers
Figure 10.3	Size of fatherhood programs
Figure 10.4	Gender of staff serving fathers
Figure 10.5	Number of survey responses

The Best Part of Being a Dad

"being capable of inciting raucous belly laughs in my child at will"

- from a father who completed the Father Involvement Survey, child's age 0-4 years

Executive summary

The value of healthy fatherhood is increasingly evident, as noted on the pages of scholarly journals, in the chambers of public policy decision makers, in classrooms for learners of all ages, and in the homes of Minnesotans of all walks of life. Research, public policy, and community life are incrementally acknowledging the need for children to experience positive relationships with men and women.

Until now, it had been difficult to view the full picture of fatherhood in Minnesota. The state had never compiled a comprehensive image of the well-being of fathers and men in families. This report adds an important perspective for us to begin seeing fathers in Minnesota.

A compendium of facts and figures about fathers: This publication is not a research report nor is it a scholarly analysis of fatherhood. Simply put, this report is a collection of facts and figures about Minnesota's fathers. By producing this compendium of information, the authors hope to shed light on the importance of fatherhood, on the need to support men in families, and on the necessity of gathering more data that tracks the well-being of all members of Minnesota's families.

Connections between child well-being and fatherhood: Through this report, the authors seek to demonstrate a two-way link between fathers' well-being and child well-being — to demonstrate vital connections between healthy fatherhood and early childhood development, community development, poverty reduction, and community well-being. In no manner is this report meant to question or undermine the importance of mothers and motherhood. Healthy fatherhood complements and supports healthy motherhood and provides children with a rich experience and understanding of life.

> **Counted versus discounted**
>
> Responses to the MFFN Survey of Father Involvement (Chapter 9) illuminate two pictures of fatherhood in Minnesota.
>
> On the one hand are involved fathers, such as the dad who described the best part of fathering: "Being the guide in their life to train, grow and learn with them about myself and teach them the values that make me what I am."
>
> On the other hand are fathers in the shadows who are uncounted or discounted in various social and legal arenas. One dad in Minnesota described the challenges of fathering: "Getting along with motherhood. Convincing the world I'm not a bad person. Trying to get time with my son."

The counted and the discounted: This report illuminates two intersecting views of fatherhood. On the one hand, the report shows that Minnesota has a healthy and involved group of men who are engaged with their children, exhibit healthy personal behaviors, and support the development of the next generation of Minnesotans. On the other hand, the report demonstrates a void of knowledge about numerous groups of fathers. These "fathers in the shadows" are uncounted or discounted in social, educational, and legal arenas. Whether due to the fathers' own choice — or due to societal coercion, neglect, and oversight — various groups of fathers are left uncounted.

Statistics illuminate intersecting views of fatherhood: Throughout this report, the statistics reveal divergent views of fatherhood: large groups of fathers who are increasingly involved with their kids versus uncounted or discounted men who have trouble connecting with their children.
- Minnesota's children ranked 3rd best in the U.S. on measures of child well-being in 2005. The link between father well-being and child well-being is still unclear. However, research shows that men and their kids benefit from positive relationships. (Chapter 1)
- Fatherhood is difficult to define. Minnesota uses more than a dozen terms to describe a man's legal or social standing as a father. (Chapter 2)

Executive summary

- More than 1/3 of Minnesota's birth fathers, in 2004, had a high school diploma, or lower levels of education. These least-educated 1/3 of fathers averaged at least 50% more children than fathers with higher levels of education. (Chapter 3)
- 6% of Minnesota's households with children are led by single men. Single father families are among the fastest growing, by percent growth, of all families with children. (Chapter 4)
- 3 of 4 custodial mothers and 2 of 3 custodial fathers received part or full child support payments due, in the U.S. in 2001. The vast majority of non-custodial parents are stepping up to support their kids. (Chapter 5)
- More than 1/2 of all state prisoners in the U.S. report having at least one minor child. Were Minnesota's prison population to resemble the national population, an estimated 4,500 fathers were housed in state correctional facilities in 2006. (Chapter 6)
- In 2004, nearly 18,000 grandparents in Minnesota had primary responsibility for their grandchildren. Among these grandparents, 36% were grandfathers. (Chapter 7)
- According to a survey of Minnesota's fathers, the most important fatherhood role is "showing love and affection" (92%) while "providing financial care" ranked lowest (76%). The survey demonstrates that many fathers focus less on their role as provider and more on their role as nurturer. (Chapter 9)
- Men comprise less than 1/3 of all professional staff working in Minnesota's social services and educational programs for fathers, according to a 2006 survey. (Chapter 10)

Recommendations for improving the well-being of fathers and families: In Chapter 11 the report includes 23 initial recommendations for future action to improve the well-being of Minnesota's fathers and families. The primary recommendations are described, in brief, here:

- **Develop a state-level office to track fatherhood health:** The State of Minnesota would benefit from a state-level office which would ensure that government agencies are tracking the health and well-being of all family members. Across the nation, a majority of states have a state-supported government agency, office, or task force on fatherhood.
- **Conduct a longitudinal study of fathers and children:** Minnesota would be well-served by a long-term study of fathers and children, from birth through adulthood. A longitudinal study of fathers and children in Minnesota would be a historic piece of research with implications for public policy, research, and social service programming.
- **Develop a mechanism for state-funding of programs that promote healthy fatherhood:** Minnesota is fortunate to have over 100 fathers' services programs. These programs, as well as programs for women and children, would benefit from a reliable state-sponsored revenue stream to help reach communities with large numbers of "fathers in the shadows" as well as underserved small towns and rural communities.
- **Address social burdens of multiple-partner fertility and unmarried births:** Minnesota would be well-served by combining early intervention and prevention policies on a cross-sectoral basis including education/job skills training, sexuality education, family planning, violence prevention, relationship skills development and marriage promotion.
- **Embrace healthy male socialization:** Minnesotans would benefit from healthy messages of manhood that prepare boys for responsible fatherhood. This would require a cultural shift to focus on more portrayals of acceptable male behaviors, less aggression, less degradation of women, more expression of emotion, and more examples of nurturing fathers.

Further research and data-collection will be important to help generate a clearer picture of areas of strength and opportunities for growth among men in families. We hope that you will scan the pages of the report to learn what we know about Minnesota's fathers, to find out what information is still inaccessible, and to decide how healthy fatherhood impacts you as a parent, a child, a community member, a taxpayer, or an advocate for healthy families and healthy childhood development.

Preface

"How are you meeting the needs of men in families?"

In 2001, the Minnesota Fathers & Families Network began to ask this question of the state's social service organizations, government agencies, educational institutions, and public policymakers. Throughout the state, your responses to this question have led to philosophical and sometimes emotional conversations about a range of topics including the roles of fathers, feminism, domestic violence, nurturant fatherhood, trends of fatherlessness, incarceration, complex family systems, young unmarried fathers, boys in educational institutions, politics, religion, and more.

In the years since we began to ask this question, we are finding more professionals interested in working with fathers, interested in learning about the value of positive father-child relationships, and interested in helping men to become a source of support for healthy childhood development.

Throughout these brief years, many of those same professionals have asked questions of us. You have asked us where to find information about Minnesota's fathers. You have asked for a profile of father involvement in Minnesota. You have asked for a better understanding of the gaps in men's services, the challenges that fathers face, and the strengths of men in Minnesota's families.

On the following pages, you will find a profile of Minnesota's fathers including indicators of the health and well-being of men in Minnesota's families.

Our answers have been passionate in support of fathers but also evasive. The truth is that we just do not know enough about men in families. Existing data can be found in isolated locations such as U.S. census figures, Minnesota School Survey results, and government agency records. When examining these data in isolation, we tend to look for information that matches our personal perceptions or professional needs. Until now, no one has compiled all of the sources of data to create a comprehensive picture of Minnesota's dads.

This report aims to provide initial answers to some of your questions. On the following pages, you will find a profile of Minnesota's fathers including indicators of the health and well-being of men in Minnesota's families. This report is a compilation of information from existing sources. In order to broaden the existing information base about Minnesota's fathers, we conducted a telephone survey of professionals who work with fathers and a survey of fathers from across the state. It is our hope that this document begins to provide a multi-dimensional portrait of the state of fatherhood in Minnesota. It is our hope that, armed with better information, we can collectively improve services for Minnesota's fathers – for the benefit of children and families in every county of our great state.

- Minnesota Fathers & Families Network, January 2007

Loren Niehoff	Dr. Glen Palm	A. Paul Masiarchin
Graduate Student Assistant	Past President of the Board	Executive Director
St. Cloud	St. Cloud	St. Paul

Introduction

Somewhere in Minnesota a father is working overtime to buy his son a bike; a grandfather is chiding his son for failure to discipline his granddaughter; a dad is driving to meet his child for their "every other" weekend together; a father in prison is drawing his young son a picture to send home; and another man is scanning the library shelves for a bedtime picture book to share with his kids.

Across Minnesota, fathers are smiling over small triumphs, struggling over daily challenges, and showing their love in small or significant ways. Like generations before – Minnesota's fathers are an integral part of countless families and all communities. Whether he is a working father or at-home dad, young parent or middle aged father, present companion or absent figure – all fathers impact the lives of their children.

Why are fathers and fatherhood relevant?

Since the early 1990s, there has been a growing body of evidence which points to the important benefits of a strong father-child relationship. Among these benefits are higher levels of school performance and increases in healthy behaviors. Fathers who are able to develop into responsible parents are able to incur a number of significant benefits to themselves, their communities, and most importantly, their children. For example, children raised with significant positive father involvement display greater empathy, higher self-esteem, increased curiosity, higher verbal skills, and higher scores of cognitive competence.[2] In 2000, the U.S. Department of Education published "A Call to Commitment: Fathers' Involvement in Children's Learning", which reveals that when fathers are involved in their children's schools, their children learn more, perform better in school, and exhibit healthier behavior.[3]

The benefits of healthy fatherhood are not relegated to one social class or one family structure. According to the same Department of Education report, "Research has shown that fathers, no matter what their income or cultural background, can play a critical role in their children's education.... Even when fathers do not share a home with their children, their active involvement can have a lasting and positive impact."[3]

On the other hand, children who lack a positive relationship with a father or father-figure demonstrate increased juvenile delinquency and lower academic achievement. "Father involvement protects children from engaging in delinquent behavior and is associated with less substance abuse among adolescents, less delinquency, less drug use, truancy, and stealing and a lower frequency of externalizing and internalizing symptoms such as acting out, disruptive behavior, depression, sadness and lying". [4]

Across Minnesota, fathers are smiling over small triumphs, struggling over daily challenges, and showing their love in small or significant ways.

Many families do not realize that the positive benefits of father-child involvement affect fathers as well as children. As explained by Frank S. Pittman, M.D., "The guys who fear becoming fathers don't understand that fathering is not something perfect men do, but something that perfects men".[5] Men, in their roles as fathers, can learn from children in the form of heightened expression of emotion, expanded sense of self, new understanding of empathy, and expanded ability for caring and nurturance.[6]

In addition to the benefits for men and children, healthy fathers recognize and honor the important role of motherhood. Indeed, fatherhood is not the opposite of motherhood and fathers are not a substitute for mothers. As stated by Rob Okun at the Men's Resource Center for Change, "I believe it is critical that men's work locate itself within the larger framework of the movement for social justice".[7] Within the context of social justice, men are encouraged to embrace fatherhood as a responsibility, as an opportunity, as a blessing.

Introduction

Healthy father-child involvement is clearly linked to the well-being of children, fathers, and families. The very presence of this link amplifies the importance of gathering data about men in families and using this information to support men to be more present, more active, and more committed to the health and well-being of their children.

How does our understanding of "manhood" impact fathering?

Any discussion of healthy fatherhood must include a glimpse at how we, as a society, are educating and socializing males to become competent fathers. Current examinations of male socialization often identify a paucity of healthy adult male role models for boys and a lack of education about what it means to grow up to become a positive man and father. In many ways, our culture fails to provide boys and men sufficient direction and support in order for individual males to define and adopt healthy expressions of masculinity and fatherhood. As this report examines the well-being of fathers in Minnesota, it is imperative that we understand the context within which boys become men and men become fathers.

As explained by anti-sexist male activist Jackson Katz, "We are raising generations of boys in a society that in many ways glorifies sexually aggressive masculinity and considers as normal the degradation and objectification of women".[8] Furthermore, Dads and Daughters, a Minnesota-based organization, has released a recent report about the stereotypes of male behavior in children's movies (the "G" rated type). The report, conducted by the University of Southern California's Annenberg School for Communication, described men as "dominant, disconnected and dangerous".[9] Men in children's movies are infrequently nurturing or caring – the roles expected of good parents. Throughout youth and adolescent culture, healthy messages of manhood that help prepare boys for fatherhood and family life are often difficult to detect.

But according to Rob Okun, masculinity is not the problem in itself. As he explains, "...gender identity can be redirected into other, more fruitful channels." He points out as an example a father that was seeking "a suitable form of rough-and-tumble play for his son that didn't involve toy guns. They hit upon firefighting and outfitted their...little boy with all the accoutrements. The ability to think clearly under pressure, to be physically strong and to take decisive action to protect others offers a useful direction to boys and young men".[7] Despite some of the prevalent negative social characteristics of masculinity, healthy manhood has a place in our families and communities.

While it can be challenging for boys to define healthy masculinity, it can be equally challenging for men to define healthy fatherhood. Christopher Kilmartin eloquently discusses the issues of fatherhood in his book, *The Masculine Self*. Kilmartin states,

> The doctrine that prescribed fathers' role as outside the home and mothers' domestic role was a result of economic exigencies that arose from industrialization. But the economy has changed and it will continue to change, increasingly making the breadwinner-homemaker dichotomy untenable, and giving rise to the different kinds of child-care arrangements that we have begun to see during the last three decades. Far from being a biologically ordained necessity, historical and cross-cultural perspectives demonstrate that the protector-provider role (in fact, all of the culturally masculine role) is a historical artifact, driven by ordinary peoples' need to make a living. From this point of view, the current debates over the 'natural' roles of women and men in the home (and elsewhere) are the 'growing pains' that come with social change.[10]

Thus, many men continue to seek appropriate family roles ranging from provider, protector, and disciplinarian to nurturer, role-model, educator, and friend. Notably, our cultural

Introduction

values about fathering have changed dramatically in just one generation. As noted by Joseph Pleck at the University of Illinois, in 1981 newly marrying couples "were asked to rank-order certain values they planned to instill in their marriages. He [found] that co-parenting – parent's sharing in the physical and emotional care of their infants and children as well as in the responsibilities and decision making" was ranked eleventh out of fifteen priorities. Upon asking the same question in 1997, Pleck found that co-parenting had climbed to the second priority.[11] Clearly, social expectations of fatherhood are changing quickly.

We hope this document can provide a touchstone for monitoring the well-being of fathers across the state – and a benchmark from which to measure in years to come.

Therefore, fathers are left asking how to define their roles. Dr. Kyle Pruett described modern fatherhood in the following terms, "Practically speaking, fathering means helping with, or paying, the bills; participating in infant care by changing diapers, bathing, and feeding; disciplining, bandaging cuts, helping with homework, driving to and from after-school and weekend activities, making trips to the pediatrician; and knowing your child's friends, passions, fears, and loves."[12] Fatherhood encompasses all of these roles but with a new emphasis on nurturing. How any one man determines and defines his own role is based on a complex set of conscious and unconscious personal and interpersonal decisions.

Does this report include all fathers throughout Minnesota?

"Do we count fathers in Minnesota?" has been compiled using a variety of source documents and resources which are cited throughout. In many cases, the report is re-packaging existing data in order to shed a light on fathers. In other cases, the report shares new insights based on two surveys: a survey about father involvement and a telephone survey of service providers conducted at St. Cloud State University for the Minnesota Fathers & Families Network. Together, these data sources provide a unique compilation about the health and well-being of Minnesota's fathers.

The report provides answers to various questions that have been researched. It also asks various questions that no one, yet, has ventured to study. In many ways, this document provides a baseline of the health of fatherhood in Minnesota. At the same time, it provides an impetus for initiating the ongoing collection of missing information on key indicators of well-being and identifying new or improved services that would support fathers.

A key finding in this report is a dichotomy of the counted versus the uncounted. On the one hand, the report shows a group of men who are engaged with their children, exhibit healthy personal behaviors, and support the development of the next generation of Minnesotans. On the other hand, the report demonstrates a void of knowledge about numerous groups of fathers. Whether due to the fathers' own choice — or due to societal coercion, neglect, and oversight — these "fathers in the shadows" are left uncounted.

Due to the multiple sources of information, "father" does not have a consistent definition within this publication. Whenever possible, the editors have attempted to focus on men, both biological and legal fathers, who have at least one child less than 18 years of age. As appropriate, the charts and tables provide different operational definitions based on the original sources and their purposes. In some cases, when Minnesota-specific data about fathers was not available, the editors included national information or general information about both parents, as a starting point.

What can I find in this report?

This document is divided into three sections. Each chapter within the report adds to a more complete portrait of Minnesota's fathers.

Introduction

Section I: Searching for Data: Research Statistics About Fathers: This section provides a factual framework for understanding Minnesota's fathers based on census data, government statistics, and indicators compiled from numerous statewide and national surveys. Within this section are facts about fathers' educational attainment, child support payments, children living in two-parent households, incarcerated fathers, child maltreatment, and much more.

Section II: Filling the Gaps: Surveys to Broaden Our Base of Understanding: The chapters in this section attempt to fill gaps in the existing data. Within this section are the responses from two surveys conducted in Minnesota in 2006. Chapter 9 looks at the responses of over 550 Minnesota fathers and their attitudes towards fathering; Chapter 10 explores social services and educational programs that serve fathers in the state.

Section III: Final Words: In this section, the authors begin to draw initial conclusions from the report and to make basic recommendations. Throughout 2007 and beyond, the Minnesota Fathers & Families Network shall utilize this report to build on our knowledge of fatherhood within our organizational work, in social services programs, and in the public and private sectors. We hope that you will join us in our effort to broaden and to implement the recommendations — in an effort to increase our understanding of fatherhood in Minnesota and to improve the well-being of Minnesota's fathers, families, and children.

This report was published by the Minnesota Fathers & Families Network. We care about children, fathers, mothers, families, and communities. We wish all children could experience the loving presence of a positive father figure. We want all men and women to understand the healthy influence that fathers can provide for the next generation of Minnesotans. We hope this document provides a touchstone for monitoring the well-being of fathers across the state – and a benchmark from which to measure in years to come.

Endnotes

[1] "Father Time: Minnesota Has Become the Epicenter of the Burgeoning Dads' Movement. Its Mission: To Encourage Men to Bond with Their Children." *St. Paul Pioneer Press*. August 21, 1994: 1G Express.

[2] Kyle D. Pruett, M.D. *Fatherneed: Why Father Care is as Essential as Mother Care for Your Child*. New York: Broadway Books, 2000: 40-54.

[3] *A Call to Commitment: Fathers' Involvement in Children's Learning*. Washington, D.C.: U.S. Department of Education, 2000.

[4] *The Effects of Father Involvement: A Summary of the Research Evidence*. Father Involvement Initiative Ontario Network, Fall 2002.

[5] Frank S. Pittman, M.D. *Man Enough: Fathers, Sons and the Search for Masculinity*. 1994.

[6] From the newsletter of the Father Involvement Initiative Ontario Network, Fall 2002.

[7] Rob Okun. "Manhood in a Time of War," *Voice Male*. Men's Resource Center for Change, spring 2005.

[8] Jackson Katz and Sut Jhally. "Put the Blame Where it Belongs: On Men," *Los Angeles Times*, June 25, 2000.

[9] Joe Kelly and Stacy L. Smith. *G Movies Give Boys a D: Portraying Males as Dominant, Disconnected, and Dangerous*. Dads and Daughters, May 2006.

[10] Christopher T. Kilmartin. *The Masculine Self, Second Edition*. Boston: McGraw-Hill, 2000: 276.

[11] Joseph Pleck. "Over the Course of Sixteen Years: Paternal Involvement: Levels, Sources, and Consequences, in *The Role of the Father in Child Development*. New York: Wiley, 1997, as quoted in *Fatherneed*, Kyle D. Pruett, M.D., 2000: 1.

[12] Kyle D. Pruett, M.D. *Fatherneed: Why Father Care is as Essential as Mother Care for Your Child*. New York: Broadway Books, 2000: 19.

section one

Searching for data

Research statistics about fathers

The well-being of Minnesota's children — Chapter 1

Context for studying the well-being of fathers

Minnesota's overall rank, 2005, based on 10 measures of child well-being: 3rd best

We know that child well-being is positively impacted by healthy fatherhood. Conversely, children who lack healthy father involvement are more likely to display higher rates of truancy, lower levels of school achievement, higher rates of teen pregnancy, and higher levels of numerous other negative indicators.

This page shows the strong indicators of child well-being in Minnesota. Although we know that positive father involvement promotes healthy children, this data begs the question: is the inverse also true? Can we make any assumptions that Minnesota's high levels of child well-being indicate a high level of positive involvement by Minnesota's fathers?

Fathers contribute to child well-being in many direct ways — interacting, teaching, role-modeling, and indirect ways — supporting mother-child relationships, providing economic support, encouraging a sense of safety. These contributions by fathers play some role in child well-being in Minnesota, but how much is difficult to assess.

Table 1.1 **Measure of the condition of children in Minnesota in 2005**	**Minnesota's rank**, among 50 states (1 = best; 50 = worst)
Percent low-birthweight babies: 2002 (babies weighing less than 5.5 pounds at birth)	5 (tied)
Infant mortality rate: 2002	6
Child death rate: 2002 (children ages 1-14)	26 (tied)
Teen death rate: 2002 (teens ages 15-19)	8 (tied)
Teen birth rate: 2002 (females ages 15-19)	6 (tied)
Percent of teens who are high school dropouts (ages 16-19)	15 (tied)
Percent of teens not attending school and not working (ages 16-19)	1 (tied)
Percent of children living in families where no parent has full-time, year round employment: 2003	4 (tied)
Percent of children in poverty: 2003	2
Percent of children in single-parent households: 2003	5 (tied)

Table 1.2 **Rank of Minnesota's neighboring states on measures of child well-being, 2005**	**Overall rank**
Iowa	8
Michigan	25
North Dakota	5
South Dakota	21
Wisconsin	10

In 2005, the top-ranked states for child well-being were New Hampshire and Vermont. The bottom-ranked states were Louisiana and Mississippi.

SOURCE: Annie E. Casey Foundation. (2005). *State profiles of child well-being: 2005 kids count data book.* Baltimore, MD: Annie E. Casey Foundation.

Chapter 2: Defining fatherhood

Across generations and cultures, fatherhood has been defined in many ways. Fathers have assumed various roles including those of provider, protector, educator, moral guide, disciplinarian, and friend. Many of these roles include the task of ensuring the passing of knowledge from one generation to another. According to Child Trends, "The types of values that parents seek to instill in their children provide the foundation and direction for their moral and ethical growth. Contemporary research suggests that the development of children's moral sense is contingent upon many factors including experiences with parents and peers and wider cultural influences."

This chapter shares facts about different types of fathers and brief definitions of fatherhood. It is interesting to note the variety of definitions and ways to identify the father of a child. The challenge of defining fatherhood raises the question: Does motherhood have the same complexity and lack of uniformity?

SOURCE: Halle, T. (2002). *Charting parenthood: A statistical portrait of fathers and mothers in America.* Retrieved January 2, 2007, from http://www.childtrends.org/Files/ParenthoodRpt2002.pdf

This information is provided for educational purposes only and is not intended to be used for legal advice. Visit www.lawhelpmn.org (click on "Family Law") for general legal information about paternity rights. For answers to specific questions of paternity and parentage, please consult a family law professional.

Table 2.1 Identifying fathers for newborns: Minnesota's birth statistics, 2004

Total number of births[1]	70,624
Births to unmarried women[1]	20,488
Percentage of births to unmarried women	29%
Approximate number of births with no father listed on birth certificate[2]	8,000 (approximate)

According to the Minnesota Department of Health, approximately 40% of all births to unmarried women do not report a father's name on the birth certificate.[2] In 2004, some 8,000 fathers are estimated to be unidentified on birth certificates in Minnesota. This number provides an approximation of the number of cases where a father would need to establish paternity, as explained later in this chapter.

SOURCES: [1] Martin, J. A., Brady, H. E., Sutton, P. D., Ventura, S. J., Menacher, F., & Kirmeyer, S. (2006). Births: Final Data for 2004. *National Vital Statistics Report,* 55(1).
[2] Minnesota Department of Health. (n.d.) *Minnesota Father's Adoption Registry Questions and Facts.* Retrieved November 2, 2006 from http://www.health.state.mn.us/divs/chs/registry/faq.htm

Brief definitions related to fatherhood in Minnesota and U.S.

The number of terms used in describing fathers represents legal status, biological connections, marital status and residential patterns. All of these factors influence the father's relationship with his child or children. They also create a complex and sometimes confusing portrait of fatherhood and do not focus on the qualities that support positive father-child relationships.

Legal father: A legal father is the man Minnesota's laws recognize as the father of the child. A legal father may or may not be the child's biological father.

Biological father: As legally defined, a biological father is the man with whom a child's mother becomes pregnant. A biological father contributes one-half of a child's genetic heritage.

Putative father: According to Minnesota law, a putative father is a man who may be a child's biological father, but who is not married to the

Defining fatherhood

child's mother on or before the date that the child was or is to be born; and has not established paternity of the child in a court proceeding.

Presumed father: In Minnesota's statutes, a man is presumed to be the biological father of a child if he and the child's biological mother are or have been married to each other and the child is born during the marriage; or if during the first two years of the child's life, he resided in the same household with the child for at least 12 months and openly held the child as his own; or if he and the child's biological mother acknowledge his paternity of the child in a writing signed by both of them and filed with the state; or if he and the child's biological mother have executed a recognition of parentage, but another man also is presumed to be the father or he was under 18 years of age upon signing the form. In certain situations, a child may have more than one presumed father until paternity is legally established.

Adoptive father: An adoptive father is a man who legally adopts a child of other parents as his own.

Step father: A step father is the husband/partner of the child's mother. The child's biological parents are the step father's wife/partner and another man, usually from a previous relationship.

Foster father: A foster father is, legally, a man who takes a father's place in the nurture and care of a child. A foster father is neither a biological father nor an adoptive father.

Social father: A social father is a cultural term for a man who takes *de facto* responsibility for a child. Social fatherhood includes "men who assume some or all of the roles fathers are expected to perform in a child's life whether or not they are biological fathers. [Social fatherhood] extends to men...who provide a significant degree of nurturance, moral and ethical guidance, companionship, emotional support, and financial responsibility in the lives of children" (*Black Fathers*, p. 6).

Psychological father: A psychological father is a cultural term usually used by academicians to describe any man who "responds to and is a significant influence in forming a child's future. Psychological fathers include friends of the nuclear and binuclear (single-parent) family, men participating in organized groups for children such as [Police Activities League], Big Brothers, and foster grandparent programs, and male teachers" (*Fathers, Sons, and Daughters*, p. 11).

Adjudicated father: A man determined by a court order or a Recognition of Parentage to be the legal father of the child. Sometimes this term is used only to refer to a father determined by a court order to be the legal father.

Custodial father and noncustodial father: A custodial father maintains legal custody of a minor child. Legal custody gives parents the right to decide how to raise their child. Parents can share legal custody of their child. A custodial father maintains primary physical care and custody of his minor child. A noncustodial father does not maintain primary care of his minor child. Custody is legally determined and is not necessarily equivalent to residency.

Resident father and non-resident father: A resident father is a man who lives in the same household as his child. A non-resident father is a man who lives separately from his child. A non-resident father may be divorced, separated or never-married to the child's mother. Residency is usually determined by the family. Except in specific situations, residency is not legally determined.

Paternity: Paternity refers to the legal father of a child. The legal father is not always the biological father. The law gives only the legal father the rights and responsibilities of a father.

Single father: A single parent is defined through marital status by being never-married, divorced, widower, or spouse absent. A single parent may or may not live with an unmarried partner or another adult. "Single", in the context of "single-parent family/household", means only one parent is present in the home.

Spouse: A spouse is defined as a person married to and living with the householder. The Federal

> Defining fatherhood is a complex task of understanding genetics, law, and social interactions.

Defining fatherhood

Defense of Marriage Act defines spouses as one man and one woman.

Householder: Households refer to the people living in a housing unit as their normal place of residence. A householder is the person, or one of the people, in whose name the home is owned, being bought, or rented. If there is no such person present, any household member 15 years old and over can serve as the householder for the purposes of the census.

Family householder versus nonfamily householder: A male family householder is a householder living with one or more people related to him by birth, marriage, or adoption. The householder and all people in the household related to him are family members. A nonfamily householder lives alone or with nonrelatives only. Individuals unrelated by birth, marriage, or adoption are classified as "nonfamilies" according to the census; this includes parents with a foster child, domestic partners, and others.

Male householder-spouse absent: This term, used by the U.S. Census Bureau, means a male householder with the wife/spouse not present. Spouse-absent includes married people living apart because of employment, away from home in the Armed Forces, moved to another area, or residing in another residence for any other reason other than separation.

Multiple-partner fertility: This term is used by researchers to describe the pattern of a man or a woman having biological children with more than one partner. In the past, this pattern generally occurred because of widowhood or widowerhood and remarriage. Today, however, increases in divorce and childbearing outside of marriage are the main factors contributing to multiple-partner fertility (Child Trends, November 2006).

Legal fathers in Minnesota

When a married couple has a child, Minnesota law automatically recognizes the husband as the child's legal father and parentage does not need to be determined. If a child's mother is not married when the child is born, the child does not have a legal father.

Establishing parentage gives a child born outside of marriage a legal father and the same legal rights as a child born to married parents.

Every child has a biological father. He is the man with whom a child's mother becomes pregnant.

Not every child has a legal father:
- A legal father is the man the law recognizes as the father of the child
- A legal father may or may not be the child's biological father

Children with legal fathers can get benefits through their fathers, including:

- Social Security benefits
- Veteran's benefits
- Tribal registration benefits
- Health care coverage
- Worker's compensation benefits
- Inheritance rights
- Children also gain by knowing both parents' biological, cultural, and medical histories

SOURCE: Minnesota Department of Human Services. (2005). *Child support-Establishing parentage.* Retrieved March 16, 2006, from http://www.dhs.state.mn.us/main/groups/children/documents/pub/dhs_id_008808.hcsp

Defining fatherhood

Establishing parentage in Minnesota

In Minnesota, an unmarried father may identify himself as the legal father of the child by signing a **Voluntary Recognition of Parentage** form (ROP). A father may use this means to establish paternity if he and the mother agree that he is the biological father and want him to be the legal father of the child. Establishing paternity by signing a ROP, in itself, does not entitle a noncustodial man to the right to parent his child. In order for an unmarried father to gain additional rights beyond paternity, a separate court action is often required to establish custody and parenting time.

Alternately, parentage may be established through legal action in court—a **Paternity Order**. Unlike a ROP, a Paternity Order can be utilized even if the parents do not agree on who the father is (a genetic test may be used to resolve conflicts). A Paternity Order will determine the legal father and will also set child support, parenting time, and legal custody.

Parentage must be established before a father's name may appear on the child's birth record.

SOURCE: Minnesota Department of Human Services. (2005). *Child support-Establishing parentage.* Retrieved March 16, 2006, from http://www.dhs.state.mn.us/main/groups/children/documents/pub/dhs_id_008808.hcsp

Putative fathers

In instances when a man believes that he may be the father of a child, he may identify himself through the Minnesota Putative Fathers' Adoption Registry as a means to gain notice if the mother were to make plans to place the child for adoption. The Fathers' Adoption Registry (FAR) strictly requires a putative father to register before the infant's birth, or within the first 30 days after the child is born.

According to the Minnesota Department of Health, the FAR was developed by the Minnesota Legislature to "provide unwed putative fathers a way to protect their interests in preserving a parent-child relationship when that child is or may be placed for adoption; and to promote stability in adoptive placements by ensuring that a child's adoptive placement is not disrupted by a putative father initiating late or untimely legal proceedings."

From 1998 through July 2002, men registered on the FAR at a rate of 33.6 registrants per year. From August 2002 through August 2005, men registered on the FAR at a rate of 63 registrants per year. These rates, while increasing two-fold, continue to demonstrate the difficulty of publicizing a process that, for many men, is misunderstood, undervalued, or simply unknown.

SOURCES: Minnesota Department of Health. (n.d.) *Minnesota Father's Adoption Registry.* Retrieved November 2, 2006 from http://www.health.state.mn.us/divs/chs/registry/top.htm

The big four questions for unmarried dads: Paternity, custody, child support and parenting time

For an unmarried or divorced father, the ability to parent his child is dependent on the peculiarities of his situation. The starting point for each father will vary depending on circumstances such as the timing of his divorce, the length of time he lived with the mother of his child, the types of documents he may have signed, the cooperation of the mother of the child, and various other situational considerations.

Due to the complexities of family law and the importance of helping all children to live in safe and healthy environments, this report does not provide comprehensive details about how a noncustodial father, presumed father, or putative father can establish a legal presence in the life of his child.

For further details, view "Unmarried Fathers' Guide to Paternity, Custody, and Parenting Time in Minnesota" online at www.mnfathers.org/resources.html and contact a family law professional for answers to specific questions.

Chapter 3: Demographic profile of Minnesota's fathers

This chapter answers the question, "Who are fathers in Minnesota?" As with any large group of the population, no "typical" father exists. There are multiple dimensions that are included in the demographic profile that combine age of father, educational level, race, ethnicity, fertility, and other factors.

A recurring theme throughout this report is the divergent information: numerous data sets count healthy fathers across the state. At the same time, various groups of men remain hidden and uncounted "fathers in the shadows."

A demographic search for information on fathers in Minnesota was conducted to illuminate what the spectrum of fathers in Minnesota might look like by accessing population data related to age, education, race/ethnicity, fertility, and related data. Results from the search exposed an expansive mosaic of multi-cultural and ethnic diversity among fathers in Minnesota, but demonstrated a lack of information about how fathers in Minnesota, and nationally, are tracked. In this chapter, and throughout the report, national data has been inserted in the absence of accessible, current statewide data. The recommendations section, at the back of this report, provides further discussion about the lack of state-level data.

Figure 3.1 **Father's age at the birth of first child**, percent distribution, U.S. 2002

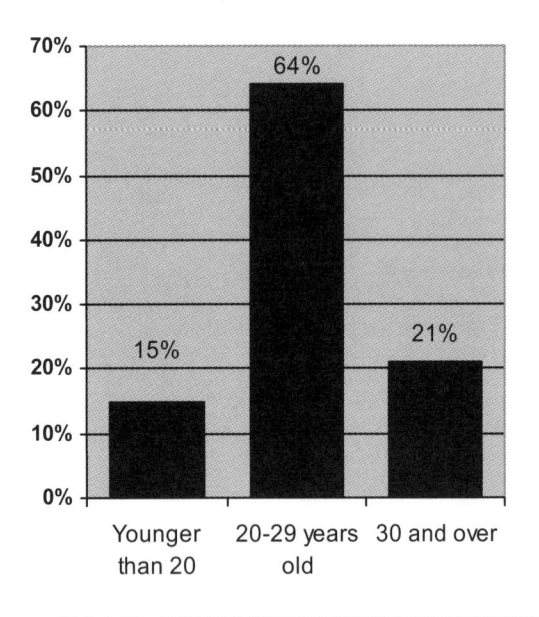

- Younger than 20: 15%
- 20-29 years old: 64%
- 30 and over: 21%

Figure 3.2 **Number of biological children fathered by U.S. men**, percent distribution of men, ages 40-44, 2002

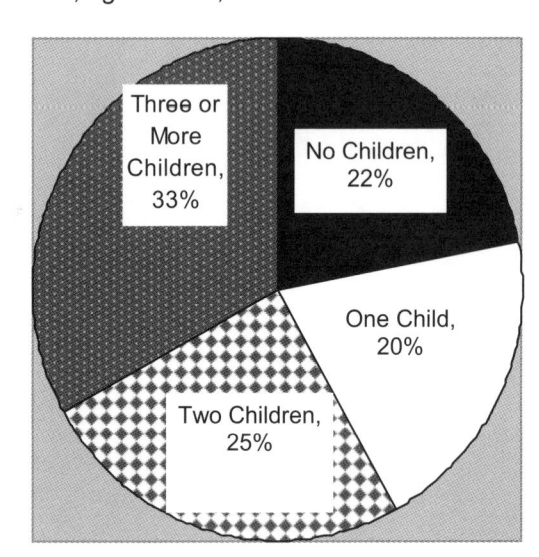

- Three or More Children, 33%
- No Children, 22%
- One Child, 20%
- Two Children, 25%

Analyzing the number of children and age of father

Figure 3.1 shows that, among fathers in the U.S., the vast majority give birth to their first child when they are between 20–29 years of age.

Figure 3.2 shows that, by the time men in the U.S. reach their early forties, one-third of all men have given birth to three or more children, one-quarter have given birth to two children, one-fifth have given birth to one child, and less than one-quarter have no biological children. The majority of adult males (78%) have at least one child by the age of 40.

SOURCE: Martinex G.M., Chandra A., Abma J. C., Jones J., Mosher W. D. (2006). Fertility, Contraception, and Fatherhood: Data on Men and Women. *From cycle 6 (2002) of the National Survey of Family Growth, 23(26).*

Demographic profile of Minnesota's fathers

Figure 3.3 **Race / ethnicity of Minnesota's birth fathers**, 2004, based on vital records of children born in 2004, where fathers' information is included

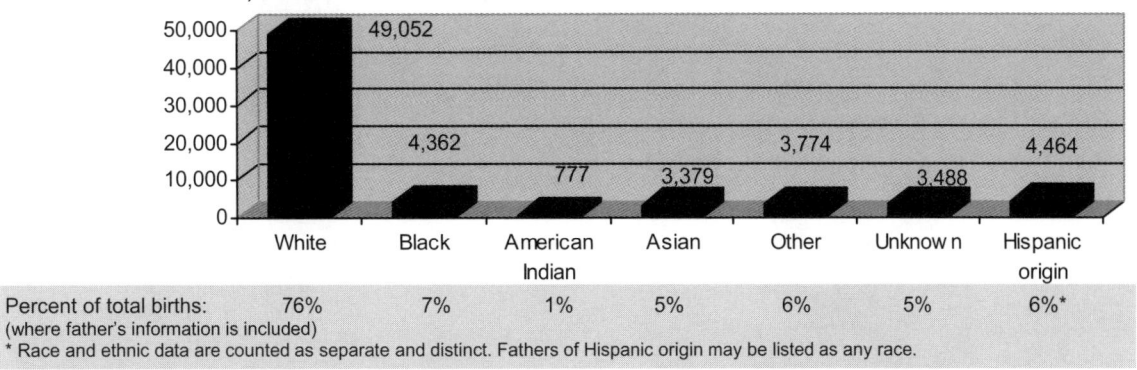

	White	Black	American Indian	Asian	Other	Unknown	Hispanic origin
Count	49,052	4,362	777	3,379	3,774	3,488	4,464
Percent of total births (where father's information is included):	76%	7%	1%	5%	6%	5%	6%*

* Race and ethnic data are counted as separate and distinct. Fathers of Hispanic origin may be listed as any race.

Birth fathers in Minnesota: 2004

In 2004, resident mothers in Minnesota gave birth to 70,624 children. Of these, 64,832 records included information on the father, included in Fig. 3.3. The fathers ranged in age from 13 years old to 80 years old. The average age of the father at his partner's first birth was 28.9 years old.

According to the National Vital Statistics Reports, "Information on age of father is often missing on birth certificates of children born to women less than 25 years of age and to unmarried women. In 2003 age of father was not reported for 13 percent of all births, 24 percent of births to all women less than 25 years of age, and 37 percent of all nonmarital births" (Vol. 54, No. 2, September 8, 2005).

Fathers' educational attainment

Figure 3.4, below, shows the educational attainment of Minnesota's men who gave birth in 2004. The numbers on this graphic coincide quite closely with the numbers on Figure 3.5 (top of following page). The main difference in numbers may be due to different divisions of education (this chart looks at post-graduate education while the above graphic looks at post-graduate degrees). On both graphs, we can see that at least one-third of Minnesota's fathers have not received education beyond a high school diploma. Indeed, the percentage of fathers with lower levels of education may be under-represented on both graphs, given the fact that a father's information is often missing on birth certificates of children born to young women.

Figure 3.4 **Educational attainment of Minnesota's birth fathers**, 2004, based on vital records of children born in 2004, where fathers' information is included

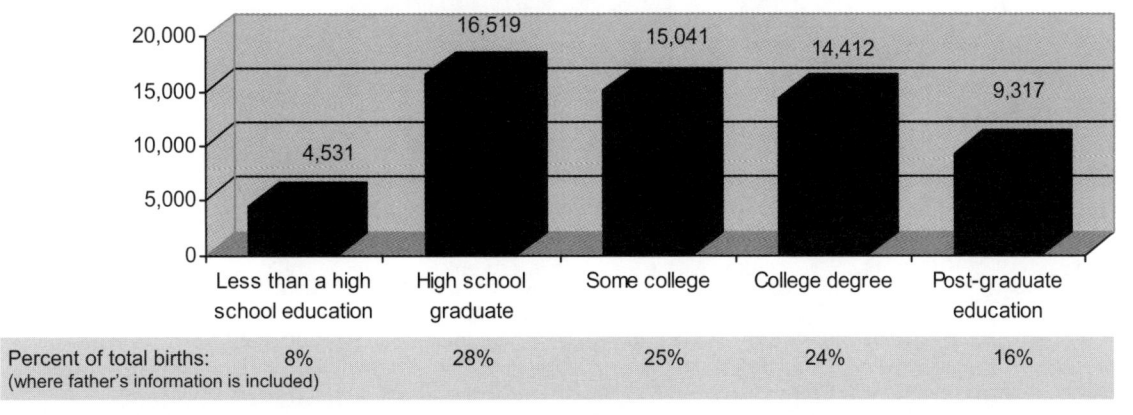

	Less than a high school education	High school graduate	Some college	College degree	Post-graduate education
Count	4,531	16,519	15,041	14,412	9,317
Percent of total births (where father's information is included):	8%	28%	25%	24%	16%

SOURCE: Minnesota Center for Health Statistics. Hajicek, C. (Personal communication, July 21, 2006). *Health Statistics.* Message sent to lorenn@albanytel.com, archived at lorenn@albanytel.com

Demographic profile of Minnesota's fathers

Figure 3.5 **Educational attainment of Minnesota's fathers**, based on fathers 25 years and older

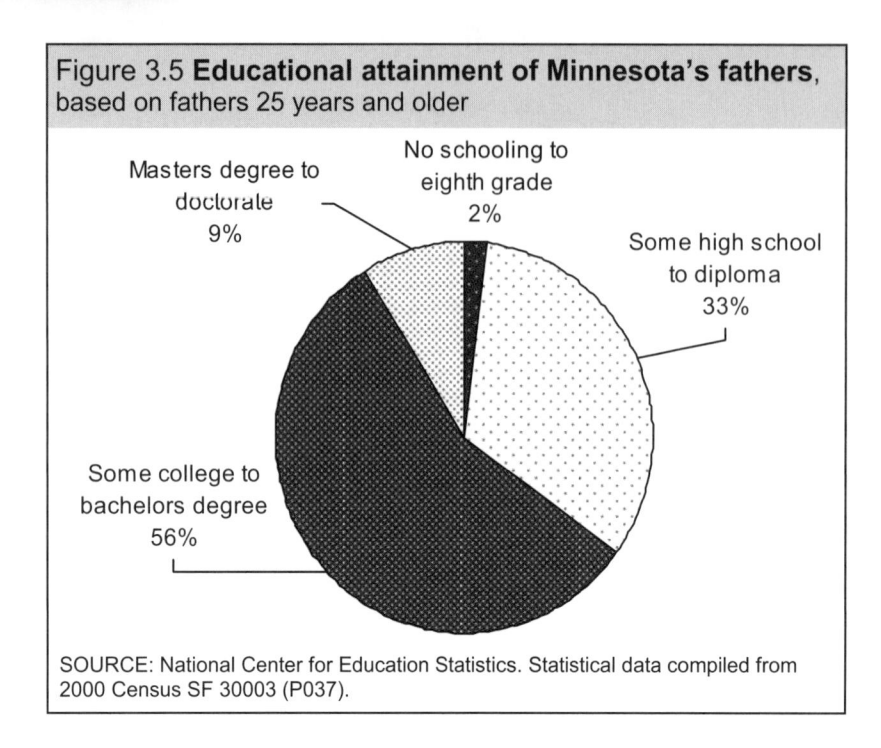

- No schooling to eighth grade: 2%
- Some high school to diploma: 33%
- Some college to bachelors degree: 56%
- Masters degree to doctorate: 9%

SOURCE: National Center for Education Statistics. Statistical data compiled from 2000 Census SF 30003 (P037).

Figure 3.6 **Fertility: Number of biological children, per man**, based on men 22—44 years of age, U.S., 2002

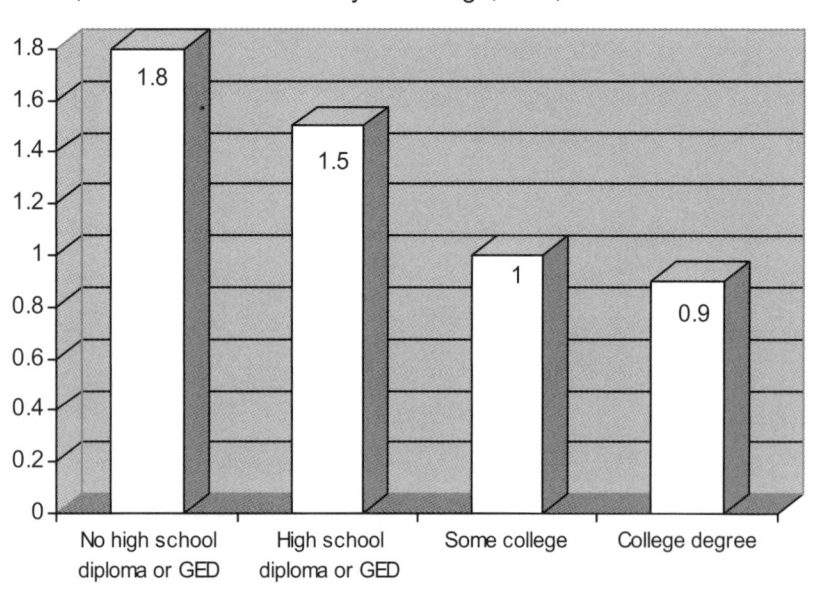

- No high school diploma or GED: 1.8
- High school diploma or GED: 1.5
- Some college: 1
- College degree: 0.9

SOURCE: Martinex G.M., Chandra A., Abma J. C., Jones J., Mosher W. D. (2006). Fertility, Contraception, and Fatherhood: Data on Men and Women. *From cycle 6 (2002) of the National Survey of Family Growth,* 23(26).

Fathers' education compared to fertility

Figure 3.5 provides a snapshot of the educational attainment of Minnesota's fathers, looking at the group of men 25 years or older who have children in the state. This data provides a glimpse of the diversity of educational background — with one-third of all fathers receiving a high school diploma or lesser levels of education, and two-thirds having completed some post-secondary education.

Figure 3.6 shows that fathers in the U.S. with lower levels of education are more likely to have already given birth to more children than their more-educated counterparts.

If these numbers are applied to the one-third of Minnesota's fathers with the lowest levels of education they are the most likely to have given birth to more than one child.

These graphs, and others in Chapter 5: Economic Indicators, raise questions about the need for additional services, especially among the state's less educated and lower income men. The graphs allude to the need to focus more on finding opportunities to close the gap in educational attainment by providing accessible educational opportunities for the state's low-income fathers. The undercounting of fathers' education level also suggests that current records may discount the need for more education for fathers.

Family structure — Chapter 4

This chapter brings together national and statewide data which conveys information about family type and how the convention of family continues to evolve. Family structure creates a context for father involvement. Evolving family structures have often been connected to absent fathers. David Blankenhorn raised the level of awareness of absent fathers in the book *Fatherless America* in 1995. He reported that 40% of children went to bed in a home where their biological father was not present.

In this chapter, national and statewide data was examined to portray the statistical parameters of fatherhood in Minnesota in relation to the type of family in which fathers are engaged. The information addresses marital status, number of children, household types, and familial trends in Minnesota. The data reflect a complex and sometimes conflicting view of family forms. Individual children and parents may experience a variety of family forms during their lifetime — moving from a marital two-parent family to a single-parent family to a blended family. The major change over the past decade has been the increase in the number of children born outside of wedlock.

According to Child Trends, "Marriage is one of the most beneficial resources for adults and children alike. Children in married parent families tend to have fewer behavior problems, better emotional well-being, and better academic outcomes, on average, than children in single parent or divorced families. Marriage is less beneficial for children's emotional and behavioral well-being in families marked by high parental conflict. Fathers' attachments to their children are often contingent upon marriage — fathers tend to disengage from children they no longer live with, making less frequent visits and calls to them over time."

> **The Best Part of Being a Dad**
>
> "Learning a different and profound aspect of life. Coming to terms with my own upbringing."
>
> - from a father who completed the Father Involvement Survey, child's age 0-4 years

Figure 4.1 **Percent of parents currently married**, U.S., comparison between biological parents, 1991 and 2001

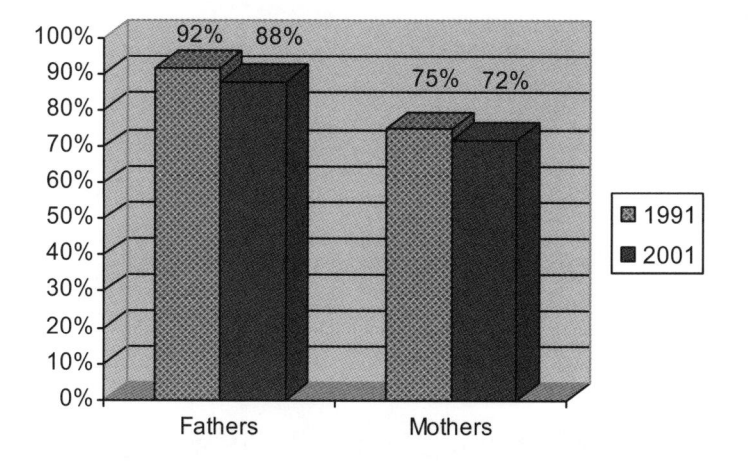

	1991	2001
Fathers	92%	88%
Mothers	75%	72%

SOURCE: Halle, T. (2002). *Charting parenthood: A statistical portrait of fathers and mothers in America.* Retrieved January 2, 2007, from http://www.childtrends.org/Files/ParenthoodRpt2002.pdf

Facts about facts: Statistics about married-couple families are easily misinterpreted

Figure 4.1 shows that fathers are more likely to be married than mothers. However, the graph does not take into account multiple-partner fertility (see Figure 4.5) which demonstrates that a man may be married — but may have had children in previous relationships. Therefore, while the statistic shows that more fathers are married, this statistic does not demonstrate how many children are living with their biological fathers in comparison to those living with their biological mothers.

Family structure

Figure 4.2 **Family groups with children under 18**, two-parent vs. single-parent households, U.S., 2000

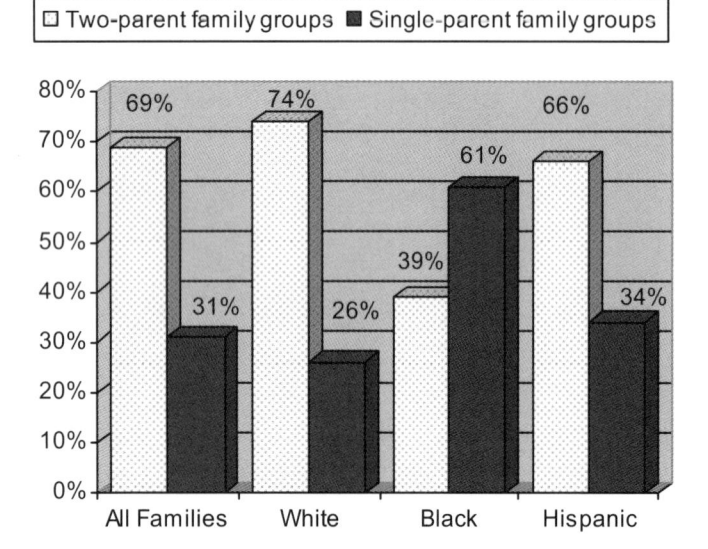

□ Two-parent family groups   ■ Single-parent family groups

Group	Two-parent	Single-parent
All Families	69%	31%
White	74%	26%
Black	39%	61%
Hispanic	66%	34%

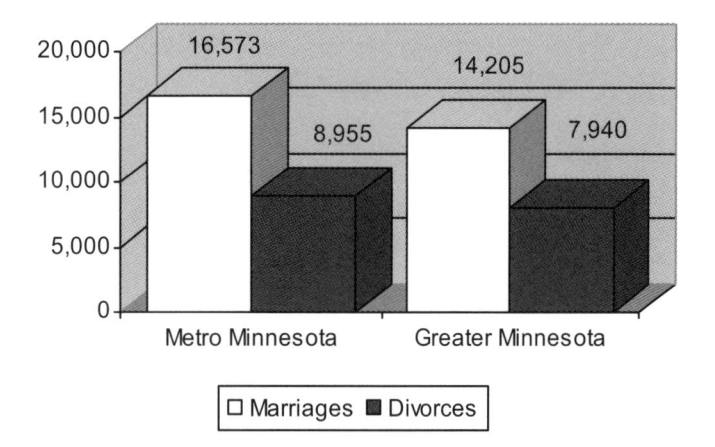

Facts about facts: Statistics about single-parent families are easily misinterpreted

Figure 4.2 shows that African-American parents are more likely than White parents or Hispanic parents to live in single-parent households. However, it is interesting to note that, among children raised in single-mother families, African-American children are *most likely to know their fathers* (as a percentage of children raised in single-mother homes). Therefore, counting the number of single-mother households is not a substitute for counting father-absent families. Figure 6.8 provides further details.

SOURCE FIGURE 4.2: U.S. Census Bureau. (2000). *America's Families and Living Arrangements* [Data file]. Available from Current Population Reports: http://www.census.gov/population/www/socdemo/hh-fam/p20-537_00.html

Figure 4.3 **Marriages and divorces**, Minnesota, 2005

Region	Marriages	Divorces
Metro Minnesota	16,573	8,955
Greater Minnesota	14,205	7,940

□ Marriages   ■ Divorces

The rates of marriage and divorce in the seven-county Metro area versus the 80-county area of Greater Minnesota are quite consistent with the total households for each area of the state, as shown in Fig. 4.3 and Table 4.1.

Table 4.1 **Statewide percentages of marriages and divorces**, by region of state, 2005

	Percent of Minnesota households	Percent of Minnesota marriages	Percent of Minnesota divorces
Greater Minnesota	47%	46%	47%
Metro Minnesota*	53%	54%	53%

SOURCE: Minnesota State Court Administrator's Office. (2005). *Marriage/Divorce Table 1 and 2*. Retrieved November 2, 2006 from http://www.courts.state.mn.us
*Metro Minnesota counties include Anoka, Carver, Dakota, Hennepin, Ramsey, Scott, and Washington.

Family structure

Figure 4.4 **Living arrangements of Minnesota's children under 18 years**, 2005

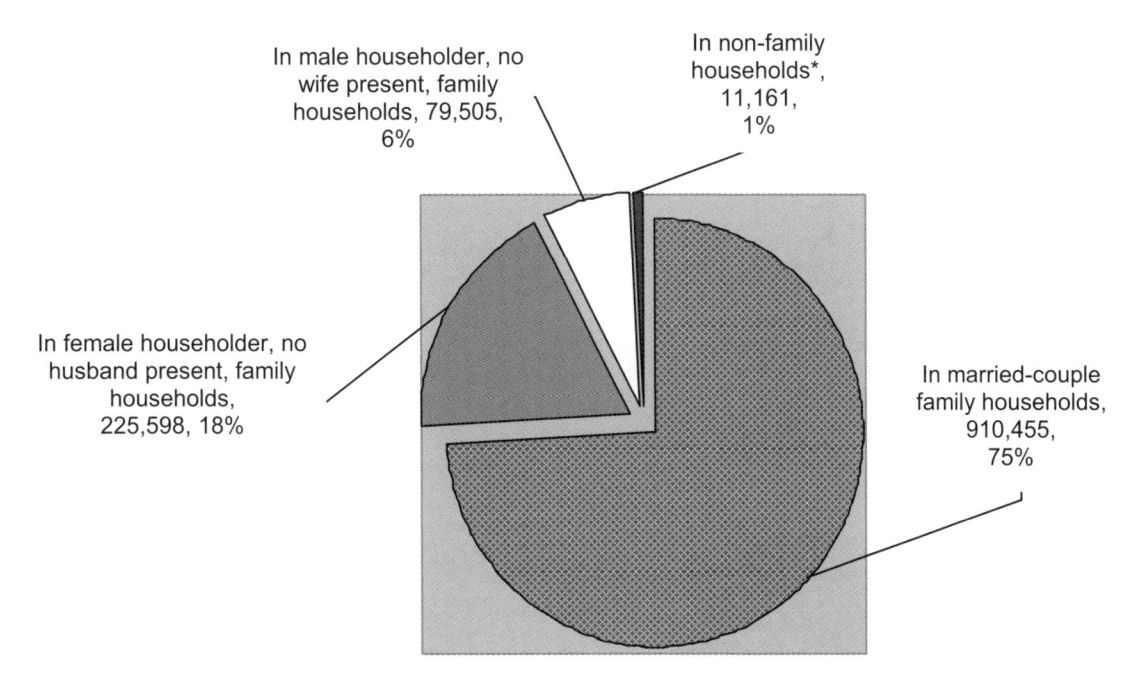

Pie chart segments:
- In male householder, no wife present, family households, 79,505, 6%
- In non-family households*, 11,161, 1%
- In female householder, no husband present, family households, 225,598, 18%
- In married-couple family households, 910,455, 75%

910,455 Minnesota children live in married-couple family households. Of these children:
- 96.3% are the biological children of the householder.
- Less than 0.1% are the householder or the householder's spouse (249 children total).
- 2.0% are the grandchildren of the householder.
- 0.9% are otherwise related to the householder.
- 0.8% are foster children or unrelated to the householder.

Among the 910,455 children living in married-couple households, these data do not reveal the full number of children living in blended families.

79,505 Minnesota children live in male householder, no wife present, family households. Of these children:
- 87.1% are the biological children of the householder.
- Less than 0.1% are the householder (35 children total)
- 2.9% are the grandchildren of the householder.
- 4.7% are otherwise related to the householder.
- 5.2% are foster children or unrelated to the householder.

Of these 79,505 children...
- 36.5% live in the presence of an unmarried partner of the householder.
- 63.5% live in a household with no unmarried partner present.

The Best Part of Being a Dad

"It's the best return on investment I've ever had."

- from a father who completed the Father Involvement Survey, child's age 0-4 years

SOURCE: U.S. Census Bureau. (2005). *American factfinder detailed tables, B09001, B09003, & B09008, 2000* [Data file]. Available from American Community Survey: http://www.census.gov/acs/www/Products/index.htm
All data are based on a sample and are subject to sampling variability.

* Nonfamily households include individuals living alone or individuals who are unrelated by birth, adoption, or marriage.

Family structure

Family structure: Percent of families with their own children, by type of family

The following two tables show the percent of total families with their own children under 18 years of age, in two family structures: married couples and single fathers. The data demonstrates that, among married-couple families with children, Minnesota ranks 4th highest nationally, behind Utah, Idaho, and North Dakota. Among single father families, Minnesota is tied for 40th place among states, slightly below the national average.

Table 4.2 **Married-couple families**, Minnesota vs. U.S., percentage of families with children, headed by married couples

Highest percentage: Utah	82.9%
Minnesota	77.4%
National average	72.9%
Lowest percentage: Mississippi	65.5%

Table 4.3 **Male-headed families**, Minnesota vs. U.S., percentage of families with children, headed by single males

Highest percentage: Nevada	9.2%
National average	6.2%
Minnesota	5.7%
Lowest percentage: Utah	4.5%

SOURCE: Office on the Economic Status of Women. (2005). *Minnesota compared to other states and the United States: Summary of the Status of Women Profile Reports.* St. Paul, MN: Author.

Facts about multiple-partner fertility*

The majority of men who have fathered children with different women were married to at least one of the women involved.

Men who have been incarcerated or have used drugs are more likely to have fathered children with more than one partner than the general male population. Approximately 61% of men who have experienced multiple-partner fertility had ever been incarcerated versus 28% of men with single-partner fertility. Similarly, 27% of multiple-partner fertility men reported using illegal drugs in the previous year versus 19% of single-partner fertility men.

Multiple-partner fertility is more prevalent among African American men. Rates of multiple-partner fertility were 32% for Black men, 14% for White men, and 17% for Hispanic men.

Figure 4.5 **Prevalence of multiple-partner fertility among men increases with age**, U.S., 2002

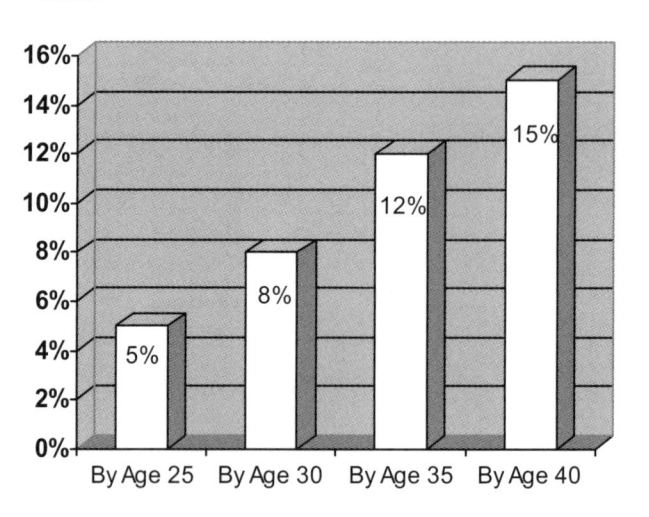

By Age 25	5%
By Age 30	8%
By Age 35	12%
By Age 40	15%

SOURCE: Logan, C., Manlove, J., Ikramullah, E., & Cottingham, S. (2006). *Men who father children with more than one woman: A contemporary portrait of multiple-partner fertility* (Publication No. 2006-10). Washington DC: Child Trends.

* The statistics about fatherhood and multiple-partner fertility are based on a nationally representative cross-sectional survey of males, ages 15-44 in 2002, with oversamples of teens, Hispanics, and non-Hispanic blacks. The data are based on 4,928 men. Of this group, 1,731 were fathers. Of this subgroup, 316 men had experienced multiple-partner fertility.

Family structure

Figure 4.6 **Marital status of Minnesota males 15 years and over**

Divorced	153,752
Widowed	37,389
Separated	15,064
Now married (not separated)	1,132,494
Never married	596,442

Various figures throughout this chapter describe family structure, and the percentages of children, students, and households living in different types of families. None of the figures, including Figure 4.6, above, provides a full picture of the living situations specific to fathers. Figure 4.6 is the only data set in this report that portrays a comprehensive view of marital status for men.

SOURCE: U.S. Census Bureau. *American factfinder, Minnesota selected social characteristics: 2004.* [Data Set: 2004 American Community Survey].

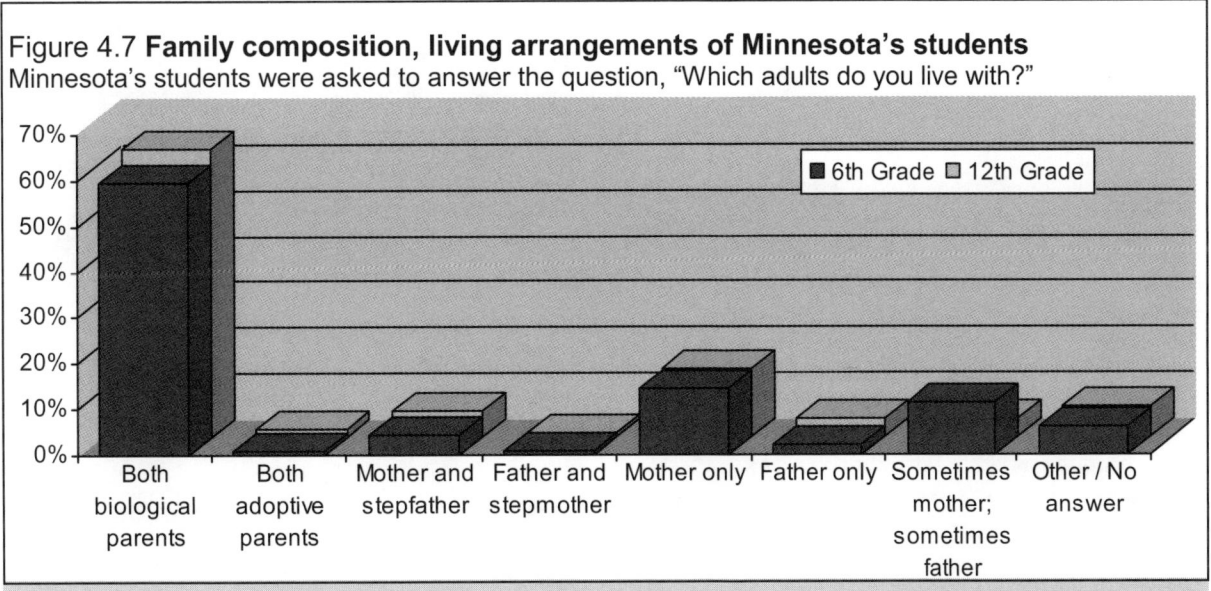

Figure 4.7 **Family composition, living arrangements of Minnesota's students**
Minnesota's students were asked to answer the question, "Which adults do you live with?"

Bar chart comparing 6th Grade and 12th Grade responses across categories: Both biological parents, Both adoptive parents, Mother and stepfather, Father and stepmother, Mother only, Father only, Sometimes mother; sometimes father, Other / No answer.

Male and female student responses in Fig. 4.7 corresponded within one percentage point except in two situations. Male 12th graders lived with their fathers at a higher rate than females (5% for boys vs. 3% for girls). Also, male 12th graders were slightly less likely to live with both biological parents (64% for girls vs. 62% for boys). The percentage of students in Figure 4.7 who do not live with both biological parents in 6th grade is 42%. This suggests that Blankenhorn's concern about children not living with their biological father on a full-time basis is a reality among 12 year old children in Minnesota, as reported in this study. (As stated on page 21, David Blankenhorn reported in 1995 that 40% of children went to bed in a home where their biological father was not present.) While biological fathers and other father figures may play a positive supportive role in the lives of these children, residential status of fathers can be a significant barrier to ongoing positive father-child relationships.

SOURCE: Minnesota Student Survey Interagency Team. (2004). *2004 Minnesota Student Survey: County Tables* (Minnesota Center for Health Statistics). annkinney@state.mn.us. Approximately 66% of all Minnesota students participated in the survey in grades 6, 9 and 12 in public operating school districts. Male and female student responses were averaged on this graph.

Family structure

Custodial parents: Marriage, employment and poverty

The figures on this page show comparisons between custodial mothers and fathers on measures of marriage, employment, and poverty.

It is interesting to note that considerably higher percentages of custodial mothers have never married, in comparison to custodial fathers. Meanwhile, currently married/widowed percentages are nearly identical.

In Figure 4.8 the data shows that both custodial fathers and custodial mothers work at high rates — with more than three-quarters of both groups employed in 2001. However, the percentage of custodial mothers employed part-time or part-year is over 50% higher than the rate among custodial fathers.

The employment statistics on Figure 4.8 provide some explanation for the poverty statistics revealed on Figure 4.9, with a higher percent of custodial mothers living in poverty.

The poverty rate among custodial mothers has dropped dramatically from 36.8 percent in 1993 to 25.0 percent in 2001. Among custodial fathers, the rate has remained fairly constant, with a 14.9 percent poverty rate in 1993 compared with 14.7 percent in 2001.

As shown in Figure 4.7, far more Minnesota students live with their single mothers than with their single fathers. Meanwhile, Figure 4.9 shows that far more single mothers, nationally, live in poverty. The impact of single parenting on rates of child poverty is an important consideration for federal and state decision makers.

National marital status of custodial parents

Custodial mothers
31.2 percent   never married
43.7 percent   divorced or separated
25.1 percent   currently married or widowed

Custodial fathers
20.3 percent   never married
56.2 percent   divorced or separated
24.5 percent   currently married or widowed

Figure 4.8 **National employment status of custodial parents**, 2001

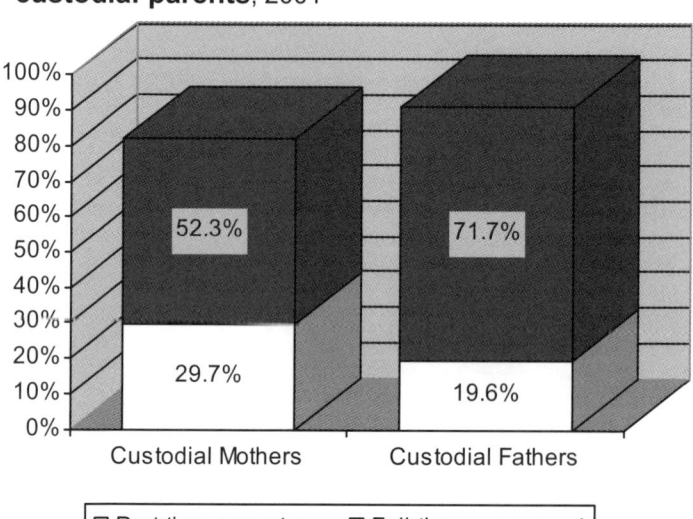

Custodial Mothers: 52.3% Full-time year-round, 29.7% Part-time or part-year
Custodial Fathers: 71.7% Full-time year-round, 19.6% Part-time or part-year

□ Part-time or part-year   ■ Full-time year-round

Figure 4.9 **National poverty rates of custodial parents**

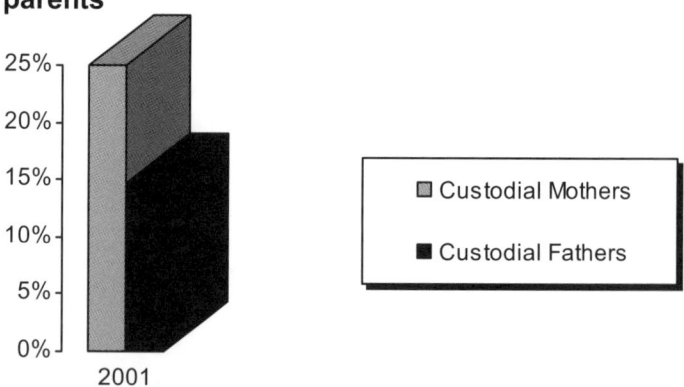

■ Custodial Mothers
■ Custodial Fathers

Source: Grall, T (2003). *Custodial Mothers and Fathers and Their Child Support: 2001*. Retrieved December 15, 2006 from Child Trends DataBank: http://www.childtrendsdatabank.org/indicators/84ChildSupport.cfm

Family structure

Minnesota's single parent families

Minnesota children and youth living in single parent families account for 21% of all households, with higher proportions in African American and Latino Families.

The number of children living in single parent families is important to note because these families may have greater needs for supportive opportunities outside the home during non-school hours. Affordability and geographic location of programs may influence access for more of these families. The large proportion of working parents with school-age children raises similar concern about the needs of these children for engaging opportunities to learn and develop during the out-of-school hours.

SOURCE: Minn. Commission on Out-of-School Time. (March 2004). *Demographic Snapshot.* www.mncost.org

Challenges for single parents

"The number of children living in households with two biological parents has been steadily declining over the past two decades and has only recently begun to level off. Although the majority of single parents are mothers, in recent years the number of single-father families has increased, accounting for 18 percent of all single parent families with children under 18 in 1998. There are several possible routes—both voluntary and involuntary—to single parenthood including getting a divorce, becoming a widow or widower, and being an unmarried parent. Regardless of the reason, most researchers agree that the fewer economic resources that single parents are able to offer and subsequent time restraints of single parenting place children raised in single-parent homes at a disadvantage."

SOURCE: Halle, T. (2002). *Charting parenthood: A statistical portrait of fathers and mothers in America.* Retrieved January 2, 2007, from http://www.childtrends.org/Files/ParenthoodRpt2002.pdf

Figure 4.10 **Children living with their single fathers**, Minnesota, 2000

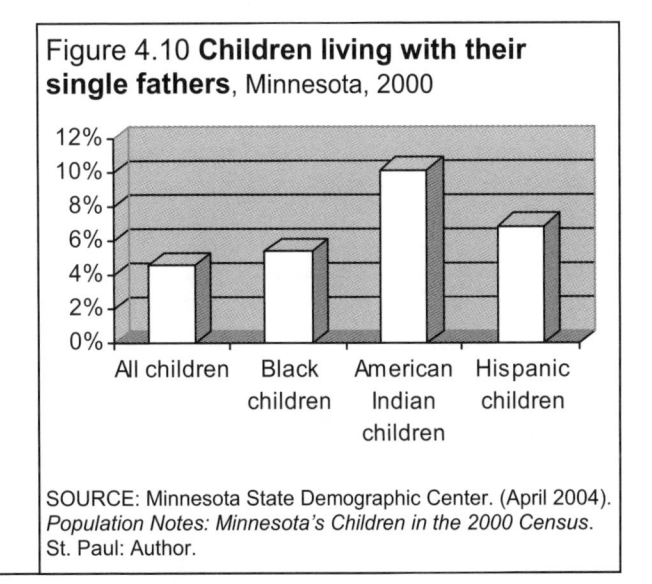

Group	Percent
All children	~4%
Black children	~5%
American Indian children	~10%
Hispanic children	~7%

SOURCE: Minnesota State Demographic Center. (April 2004). *Population Notes: Minnesota's Children in the 2000 Census.* St. Paul: Author.

Figure 4.11 **Father closeness and adolescent drug abuse: The impact of family structure**

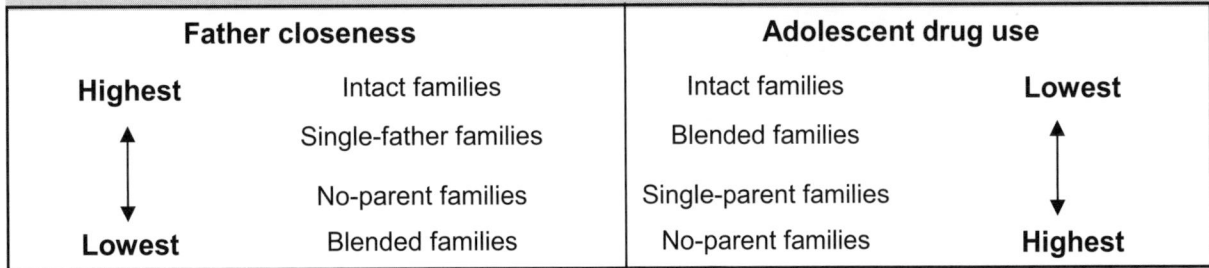

Father closeness		Adolescent drug use	
Highest ↑ ↓ **Lowest**	Intact families Single-father families No-parent families Blended families	Intact families Blended families Single-parent families No-parent families	**Lowest** ↑ ↓ **Highest**

According to a report by the National Fatherhood Initiative, "certain family structures tend to produce lower levels of risk for adolescent drug use, with an emphasis on the role that father involvement plays in helping adolescents avoid risky behavior." The report goes on to report, "Given that father closeness reduces adolescent drug use, and that father closeness is highest in intact families, adolescents in intact families are at the lowest level of risk for engaging in drug use." Findings from the report verified that family structures tend to play a role in adolescent drug use, as noted in Figure 4.11.

SOURCE: National Fatherhood Initiative. (2004). *Family Structure, Father Closeness, & Drug Abuse.* Gaithersburg MD. Retrieved March 10, 2006, from http://www.fatherhood.org/research.htm

Family structure

Figure 4.12 Minnesota household projections, 2000—2030

- Male Householder: 37,305 (2000 Census), 57,900 (2030 Projections)
- Female Householder: 111,371 (2000 Census), 135,600 (2030 Projections)

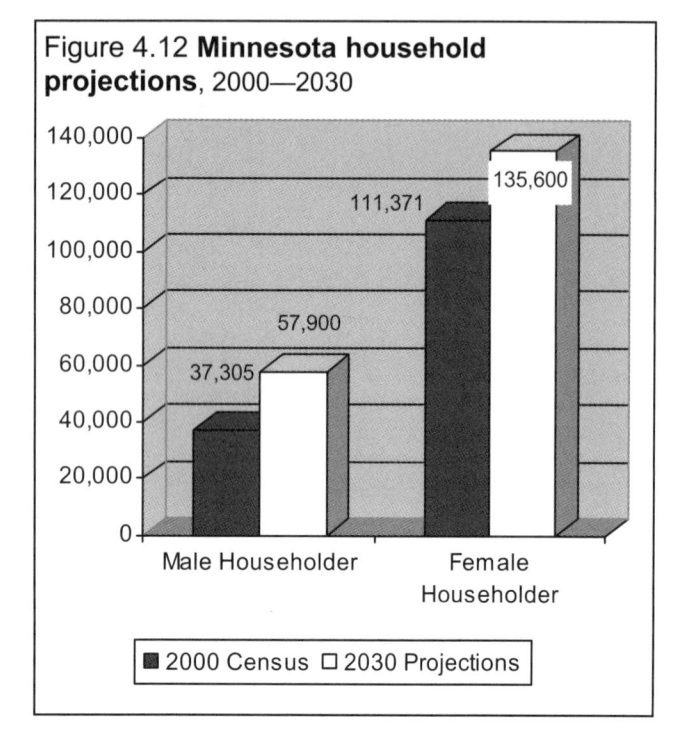

Figure 4.13 Minnesota projected change in type of households, 2000—2030

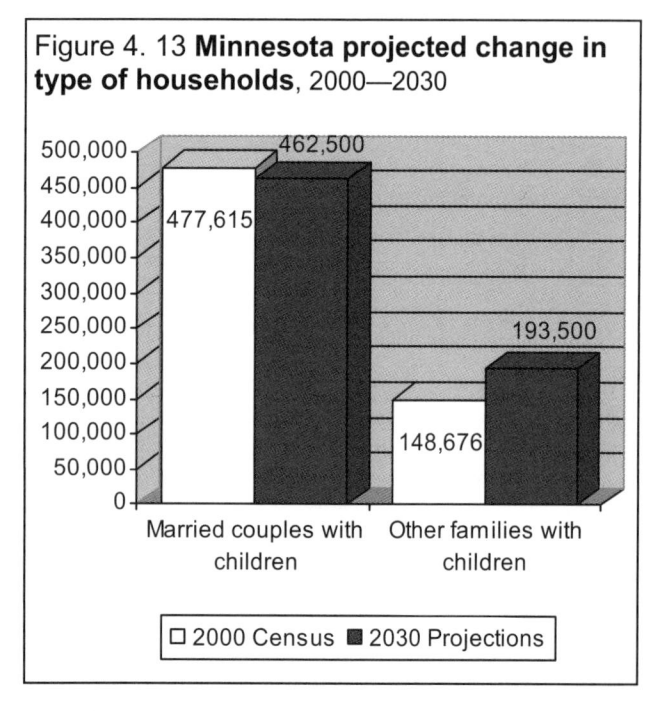

- Married couples with children: 477,615 (2000 Census), 462,500 (2030 Projections)
- Other families with children: 148,676 (2000 Census), 193,500 (2030 Projections)

SOURCE: Minnesota Department of Administration State Demographic Center (2003). *Minnesota household projections 2000-2030.* Retrieved January 2, 2007, from http://www.demography.state.mn.us

Future projections: Number of other families with children will grow at a moderate rate

The data in Fig. 4.13 shows a relatively stable number of married couple households with children and a growing number of other families with children. Projections of changes in Minnesota's households leading up to 2030 show a modest decline in the number of married couples with children (3% decline) juxtaposed against moderate growth in other families with children (23% increase).

"The number of single parent families has risen dramatically in recent decades. The projections in Fig. 4.12 show this household type will grow, but at a rate slightly below the overall rate of household growth. In the decade from 2000 to 2010, the number of single mother families is projected to grow by about 11,000 and the number of single father families by about 10,200. In 2000, 24 percent of households with children were single-parent households. This will increase to 27 percent by 2010 and 30 percent by 2020."

In 2000, the percent of single father households was 6% of all families while single mother households made up 18% of all families. Between 2000 and 2030, single father families will increase by approximately 55% while single mother families will increase by 21%.

Economic Indicators — Chapter 5

In this chapter, the data sheds a light on the economic factors that impact each father's ability to provide for his family's material needs and financial stability.

How are fathers in Minnesota doing financially to provide for their families? A look at economic factors in Minnesota postulates a correlation between a father's economic stature and his ability to provide economically for his family. Income, employment status, and health care coverage supply economic data about what is happening and available to the fathers of Minnesota. This chapter also briefly explores workplace policies, including the availability of father-friendly leave policies and employment benefits that support working families.

Family structure also demonstrates correlations to family income, with higher percentages of single-parent families experiencing conditions of poverty. A family's participation in child support, child care services, and additional programs can impact the finances available for other household priorities. Additionally, many of the data sets fail to take into consideration multiple-partner fertility; for fathers who have children living in more than one household, economic support is often stretched in different directions.

Table 5.1 **Employment status: Percent of both parents or single parent in the labor force**, 2000, based on families with children under six years old

Highest: S. Dakota	73.0%
Minnesota	68.8%
National average	58.6%
Lowest: California	51.8%

Minnesota ranked fifth highest in the U.S. on this indicator in 2000, behind South Dakota, North Dakota, Iowa, and Nebraska. Wisconsin, the only other state bordering Minnesota, ranked 6th nationally.

Figure 5.1 **Family income and earnings**, Minnesota vs. U.S., median income based on family structure, families with children under 18 years old, 2000

SOURCE: Office on the Economic Status of Women. (2005). *Minnesota compared to other states and the United States: Summary of the Status of Women Profile Reports.* St. Paul, MN: Author.

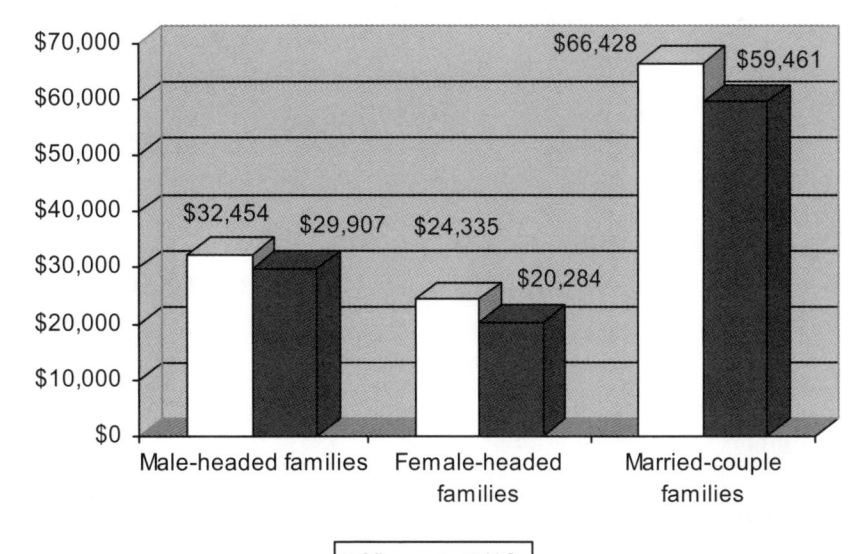

Family structure	Minnesota	U.S.
Male-headed families	$32,454	$29,907
Female-headed families	$24,335	$20,284
Married-couple families	$66,428	$59,461

Economic Indicators

Poverty and marriage: According to Child Trends, "Only 41 percent of poor men were married in 2001, and as income rises, so does one's probability of being married, such that 66 percent of men living at 300 percent of the poverty level were married in 2001."

Table 5.2 Minnesota parental education and economic security
When parents have lower levels of education, their families are more likely to live in poverty.

Percent of families with parents with no high school degree	4%
Percent of families with parents with no high school degree who are low income	69%
Percent of families with parents with only a high school degree	17%
Percent of families with parents with only a high school degree who are low income	44%
Percent of families with parents with education beyond high school	79%
Percent of families with parents with education beyond high school who are low income	14%

SOURCE: National Center for Children in Poverty. (2005). *Family Economic Security: Minnesota State Context.* Retrieved March 20, 2006, from http://www.nccp.org/state_detail_Context_MN.html

Figure 5.2 Rental housing: Percent of families renting their homes, by type of household, Minnesota, 2000

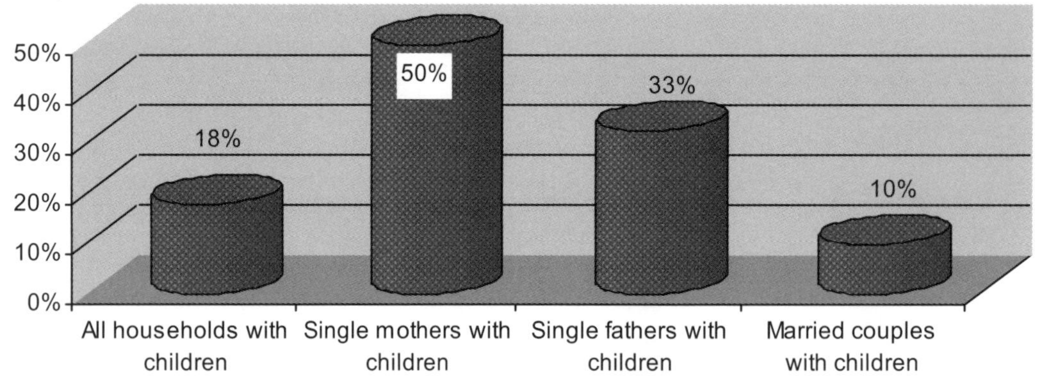

- All households with children: 18%
- Single mothers with children: 50%
- Single fathers with children: 33%
- Married couples with children: 10%

Rental housing by families with children, by Minnesota county

The counties with the highest rates of rental housing, among families with children, include Hennepin, Ramsey, and numerous counties throughout Greater Minnesota. The counties with the lowest rates include Lake of the Woods, Roseau, Marshall, Houston, and the majority of the suburban counties: Washington, Chisago, Isanti, Sherburne, Wright, McLeod, Carver and Scott.

SOURCE: Children's Defense Fund Minnesota. (2000). *Minnesota Children and the 2000 Census: Housing and Families.* Retrieved March 12, 2006 from http://www.cdf-mn.org/CensusData2000/MNChildHousing.pdf

Economic Indicators

Child support in Minnesota: Facts and figures

more than 407,000	Custodial and noncustodial parents who were provided services by county and state child support offices.[1]
174,102	Children who received a collection, either current child support and/or arrears, in the federal fiscal year ending 9/30/2006.[2]
268,233	Children in Minnesota's statewide child support caseload as of 9/30/2006.[2]
about 161,000	Children born outside of marriage who have a Minnesota child support case.[1]
96%	Percent of children born outside of marriage for whom paternity has been established, as of September 2005.[1]
at or above 80%	Overall paternity establishment rate which states must maintain in order to receive full federal incentives. States must also pass a data reliability audit for this measure.[1]

SOURCE: [1]Minnesota Department of Human Services. (n.d.). *Child Support in Minnesota: Facts and figures.* Retrieved January 2, 2006, from http://www.dhs.state.mn.us
[2] Minnesota Department of Human Services. Campbell, W. (Personal Communication, December 14, 2006). *Child Support Enforcement Division.* Message sent to info@mnfathers.org, archived at info@mnfathers.org

Figure 5.3 Minnesota child support collections by source, state fiscal year 2005

- Income Withholding: 72%
- Other Sources: 14%
- Other States: 6%
- Federal Tax Intercept: 3%
- State Tax Intecept: 2%
- Unemployment Insurance: 3%
- Administrative Enforcement: 0%

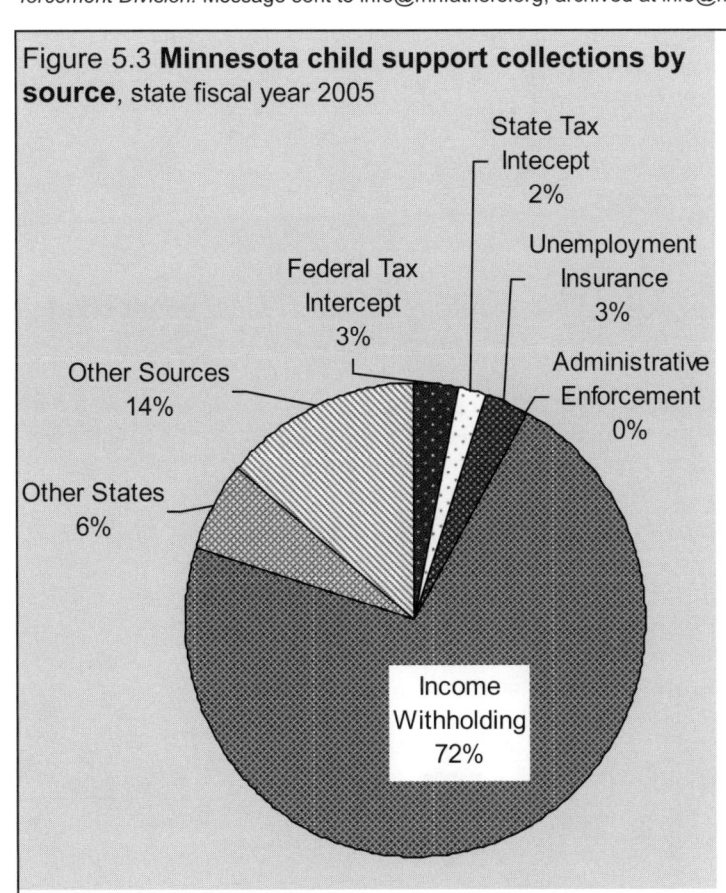

Income withholding is achieved by employers withholding child support obligations from the paycheck of a noncustodial parent. When parents owe past due support, federal and state tax intercepts are important sources of collections.

Minnesota child support 2005

Disbursements: $595 million
Open Cases: 249,346

Dollars collected per child support case, federal fiscal year 2004

Minnesota: $2,303
National: $1,379
Minnesota's rank, nationally: 3rd highest

Paternity establishment in Minnesota by federal fiscal year, based on open child support cases

2000	74%
2002	82%
2004	98%

Paternity establishment rates are calculated by taking the number of children in open IV-D (child support) cases with paternity established and dividing by the number of children in open IV-D cases born outside of marriage.

Source: Minnesota Department of Human Services. (2005). *2005 Minnesota child support: Performance report* (Child Support Enforcement Division). Retrieved March 1, 2006, from http://www.dhs.state.mn.us

Economic Indicators

Figure 5.4 **Percent of custodial parents awarded child support**, 2002, U.S.

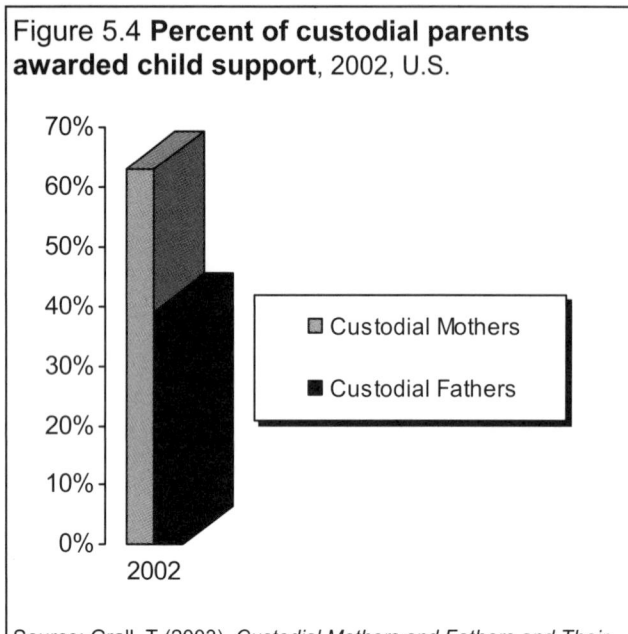

[Bar chart showing Custodial Mothers at approximately 63% and Custodial Fathers at approximately 39% for 2002]

Source: Grall, T (2003). *Custodial Mothers and Fathers and Their Child Support: 2001*. Retrieved December 15, 2006 from Child Trends DataBank: http://www.childtrendsdatabank.org/indicators/84ChildSupport.cfm

Minnesota's collections on current child support obligations

2000	68%
2002	72%
2004	69%

Lowest rate of collections (50-59%):
   Mahnomen Co., Cass Co.

Highest rate of collections (80-89%):
   Roseau Co., Lake of the Woods Co.

Collections on current support rates are calculated by taking the total amount of support distributed as "current support" during the year, and dividing by the total amount of current support due. "Current support due" is the total dollars due in current support obligations, as opposed to arrears.

Source: Minnesota Department of Human Services. (2005). *2005 Minnesota child support: Performance report* (Child Support Enforcement Division). Retrieved March 1, 2006, from http://www.dhs.state.mn.us

---

Across the U.S., about three-quarters of custodial parents received at least some child support payments.

"Approximately 6.9 million of the 7.9 million custodial parents with child support agreements or awards in 2002 were due payments from those awards. Among these parents who were due support in 2001, 73.9 percent received at least some payments directly from the noncustodial parent."

Figure 5.5 **Custodial parents receiving part or full child support payments due**, 2001

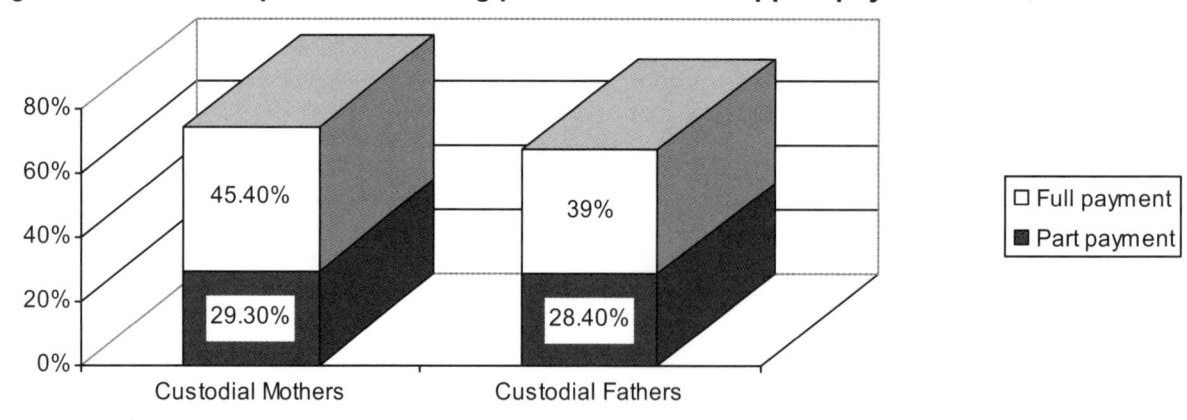

[Bar chart:
- Custodial Mothers: Full payment 45.40%, Part payment 29.30%
- Custodial Fathers: Full payment 39%, Part payment 28.40%]

Source: Grall, T (2003). *Custodial Mothers and Fathers and Their Child Support: 2001*. Retrieved December 15, 2006 from Child Trends DataBank: http://www.childtrendsdatabank.org/indicators/84ChildSupport.cfm

Economic Indicators

Nonpayment of child support

Noncustodial mothers and fathers fail to pay child support at nearly equal rates. "These findings of nonsupport among noncustodial [parents] suggest that there is something in the structure of nonresidential parenting...which is the principal inhibitor of economic support for children outside of marriage. Structural aspects of nonresidential parenting that may inhibit economic support might include having to send funds to an ex-spouse, or ex-partner, having to provide economic support in the absence of day-to-day contact with one's children, and having no influence over how child support funds are spent."

SOURCE: Doherty, W. J., Kouneski, E. F., & Erickson, M. F. (1996). *Responsible Fathering: An overview and conceptual framework.* (HHS-100-93-0012). Washington DC: Administration for Children and Families.

Table 5.3 Stay-at-home fathers

5.5 million	Stay-at-home parents in the U.S. in 2003, estimated
98,000	Stay-at-home fathers in the U.S.
29%	Stay-at-home dads with their own children under 3 years of age living with them
30%	Stay-at-home dads under age 35

SOURCE: U.S. Census Bureau. (2004). *Stay at home parents top 5 million* [Data file]. Available from Census Bureau Reports: http://www.census.gov/Press-release/www/releases/archives/families_households/003118.html.

Figure 5.6 Fathers' health care coverage, based on percentage of children, Minnesota vs. U.S.

Percentage of children living with fathers who have health care coverage. Children/youth ages 0 - 17 years who live with their biological, step, foster or adoptive fathers. Nationally, about 74% of children had a biological, step, foster or adoptive father in the household.

SOURCE: National Survey of Children's Health. (2005). *Child and adolescent health measurement initiative.* Retrieved July 10, 2006 from http://www.nschdata.org/content/ChartbooksPubsAndPresentations.aspx

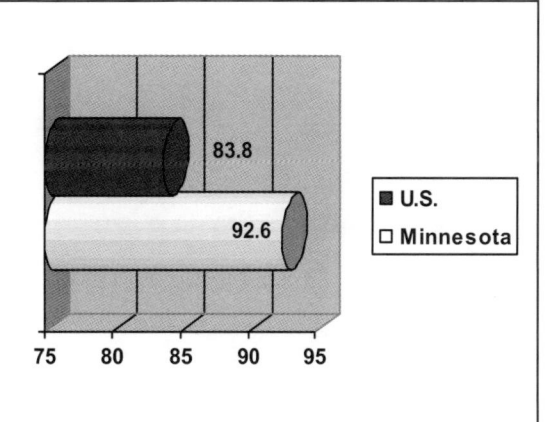

- U.S.: 83.8
- Minnesota: 92.6

Figure 5.7 Minnesota male-headed families: Health care coverage, by family status, no spouse present, numbers of male-headed primary families insured vs. uninsured (based on male-headed families with no spouse present)

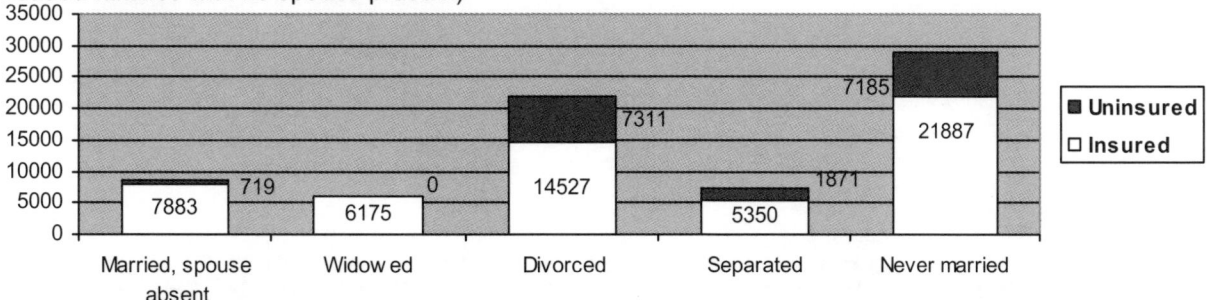

Family Status	Insured	Uninsured
Married, spouse absent	7883	719
Widowed	6175	0
Divorced	14527	7311
Separated	5350	1871
Never married	21887	7185

SOURCE: U.S. Census Bureau, (2005). Current population survey 2005. Retrieved March 15, 2006, from http://www.census.gov

Economic Indicators

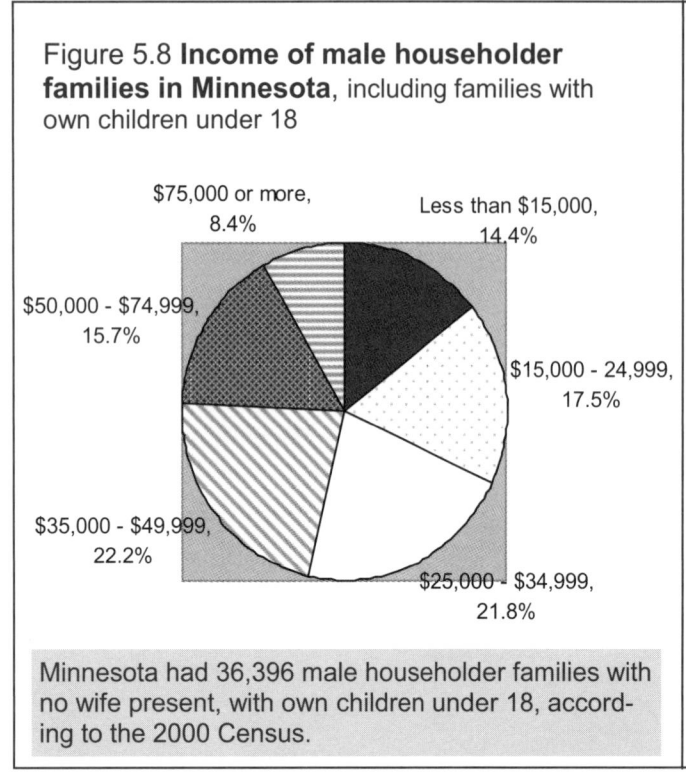

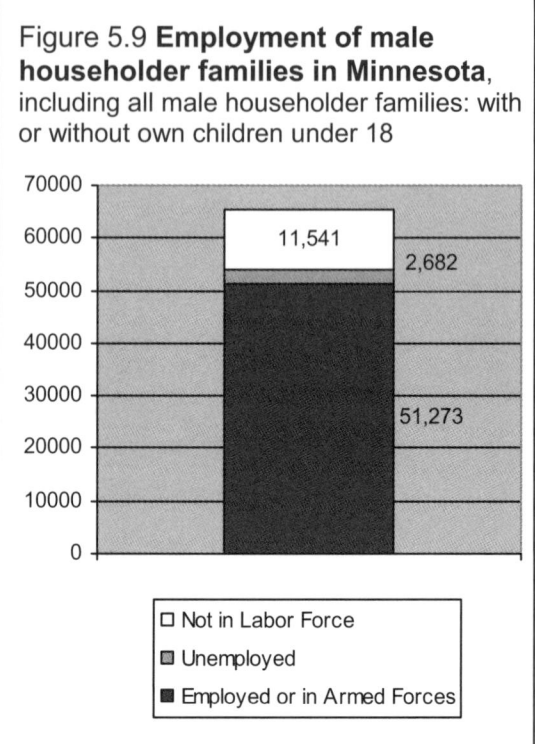

Figure 5.8 **Income of male householder families in Minnesota**, including families with own children under 18

- $75,000 or more, 8.4%
- Less than $15,000, 14.4%
- $50,000 - $74,999, 15.7%
- $15,000 - 24,999, 17.5%
- $35,000 - $49,999, 22.2%
- $25,000 - $34,999, 21.8%

Minnesota had 36,396 male householder families with no wife present, with own children under 18, according to the 2000 Census.

Figure 5.9 **Employment of male householder families in Minnesota**, including all male householder families: with or without own children under 18

- Not in Labor Force: 11,541
- Unemployed: 2,682
- Employed or in Armed Forces: 51,273

SOURCE: U.S. Census Bureau (2000). Retrieved from State of Minnesota SF3—PCT38, www.state.mn.us

Minnesota Family Investment Program: Families receiving welfare

In 2004, combined federal and state spending for welfare food and cash assistance in Minnesota was $319 million for an average of 44,000 families monthly.

Among Minnesota's welfare recipients, from 2000 through 2005, approximately 20% of all cases have consistently been led by two parents/caregivers.

However, the number of male recipients has grown dramatically, as a percentage of cases, since Minnesota instituted changes under MFIP which allowed two-parent families to receive welfare support, as shown in Figure 5.10.

Figure 5.10 **Men receiving welfare, as percent of eligible adults on Minnesota's MFIP program**, 1997—2005

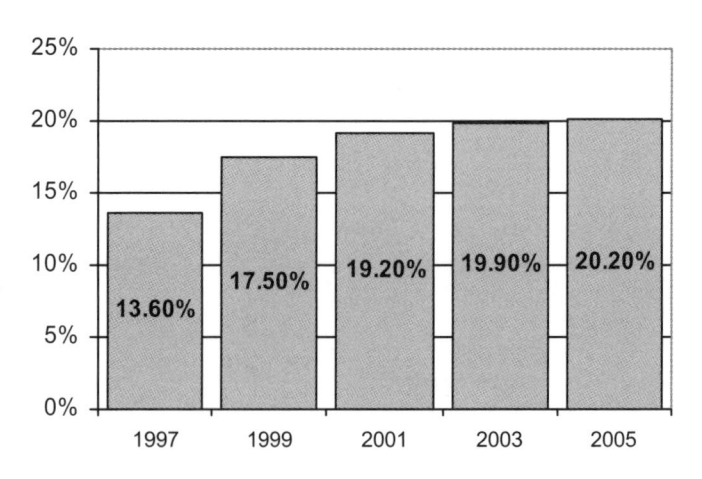

Year	Percent
1997	13.60%
1999	17.50%
2001	19.20%
2003	19.90%
2005	20.20%

SOURCE: Minnesota Department of Human Services. Chazdon, S. (Personal Communication, December 15, 2006). *Program Assessment and Integrity Division*. Message sent to info@mnfathers.org, archived at info@mnfathers.org. Figures for 1997 are from the AFDC program. MFIP became Minnesota's welfare program in 1998. Figures for 2005 include MFIP and the Diversionary Work Program, developed to divert families from welfare by offering them 4-months of financial support and employment services.

Economic Indicators

Table 5.4 **Income adequacy in Minnesota**

- Percent of families with low incomes[1]	21%
- Percent of families who are officially poor[2]	8%
- Children with at least one parent working full-time, who are low income	16%
- Median annual income for family of 4	$76,733
- U.S. federal poverty guidelines, 2006, for a family of 4	$20,000
- State rank in income inequality (50 is most unequal)	9

SOURCE: National Center for Children in Poverty. (2005). *Family Economic Security: Minnesota State Context.* Retrieved March 20, 2006, from http://www.nccp.org/state_detail_Context_MN.html
[1] Figure reflects the percent of families with annual income below 200 percent of the poverty level.
[2] Figure reflects the percent of families with annual income below the poverty level.

The question of minimum wage

Minnesota's minimum wage of $6.15 per hour is $1.00 more than the federal minimum (as of November 2006). Nonetheless, 16% of children are low income despite having at least one parent who works full-time.

Work-life policies in Minnesota

"The ability of families to fulfill their basic functions of family creation, economic support, child rearing and caring for their members is significantly influenced by the roles, options and policies the adults in the family have at their places of employment.

"The U.S. lags far behind many other industrialized nations in its policy supports for working families. More parents are covered by leave policies and they receive a much higher level of salary replacement during leaves in many other countries. For instance, a recent report from the Harvard School of Public Health found that 160 countries offer guaranteed paid leave to women in connection with childbirth. The U.S. does not.

"The federal Family and Medical Leave Act of 1993 requires employers with 50 or more employees to allow some employees to take up to 12 weeks of unpaid leave for specific purposes. The federal law technically does not include the common illnesses of young children, although some employers do allow for them. Some states have augmented FMLA with additional leave policies. For instance, California is currently the only state that provides paid family leaves to mothers, fathers, and those caring for sick relatives.

"Minnesota enhances FMLA with its Minnesota Parental Leave Law, that requires smaller employers with 21 or more employees to provide unpaid leave to mothers and fathers upon the birth or adoption of a child. In addition, employers with 21 or more employees must allow parents who are employed at least half-time to use their paid sick leave to care for their own sick child, including common illnesses. And all workers in Minnesota, regardless of the size of the employer, must be allowed to take up to 16 hours per year of unpaid leave to attend school, child care, or other activities of their children. These additional policies put Minnesota in the top 20% of states' policies on family leave, according to one ranking by the National Partnership for Working Families."

SOURCE: Kelly, E (2005). The impact of work-life policies on families. *Consortium Connections.* 14 (1).

> **The Most Challenging Part of Being a Dad**
>
> "being consistent in communication and discipline, especially when I'm tired or distracted"
>
> - from a father who completed the Father Involvement Survey, child's age 0-4 years

Chapter 6: Barriers to father involvement

This chapter explores a variety of the circumstances that create challenges and barriers that may impede positive father involvement. Each of these circumstances may diminish a father's ability to focus on the well-being of his family and child. Many of these "edge issues" create a separation — such as physical distance or emotional distance — which inhibits positive daily father-child interactions.

Although various measures of father well-being are grouped together in this section, each circumstance is unique in its affect on fathers and children. This chapter does not intend to imply any similarity between military service and incarceration — or any of the other circumstances described here — beyond the fact that each one impacts a father's ability to be positively engaged with his children.

America's incarcerated fathers

By the end of 2002, 1 in 45 minor children had a parent in prison. These children represent 2 percent of all minor children in America [about 1.5 million], and a sobering 7 percent of all African-American children. More than half of all state prisoners in the U.S. reported having at least one minor child. "Because far more men than women are sent to prison each year, our criminal justice policies have created a 'gender imbalance', a disparity in the number of available single men and women in many communities." In communities with high rates of incarceration, "young women complain about the shortage of men who are suitable marriage prospects because so many of the young men cycle in and out of the criminal justice system. The results are an increase in female-headed households and narrowed roles for fathers in the lives of their children."

SOURCE: Travis, J. (2005). *But they all come back: Facing the challenges of prisoner reentry*. Washington, DC: The Urban Institute Press.

Minnesota's inmate population: Where are the fathers?

According to the 2006 Minn. Department of Corrections Adult Inmate Profile, the state agency gathers information on the following inmate characteristics: gender, offenses committed, average age, number of inmates 50 years of age or older, number of inmates under age 18, inmates certified as adults at sentencing, race, educational level, marital status, religion, and various other facts. However, the Department of Corrections keeps no official records about the parenthood of offenders.

Figure 6.1 **Minnesota Department of Corrections adult inmate population** as of 01/01/2006

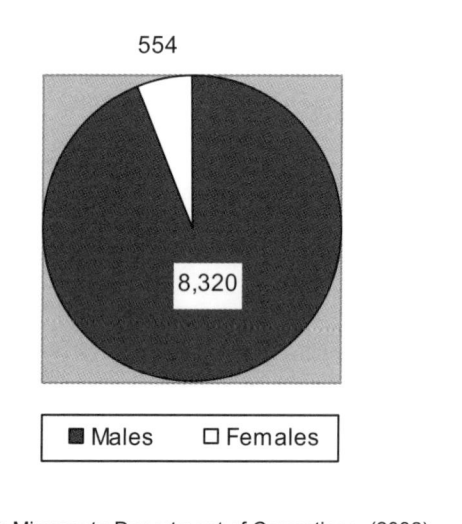

554
8,320

■ Males   □ Females

SOURCE: Minnesota Department of Corrections, (2006). Adult inmate profile as of 1/01/2006. Retrieved March 20, 2006, from http://www.doc.state.mn.us

Estimating Minnesota's incarcerated father population

The national average of fatherhood among incarcerated men in state prisons is 55% (men with children under 18 years old).

The Minn. Department of Corrections housed 8,320 adult men in 2006.

Therefore, were Minnesota's state prison population to resemble the national population housed in state prisons, **the state would have had approximately 4,576 fathers in state correctional facilities.**

Barriers to father involvement

Table 6.1 **Children and families of military personnel**, Minnesota and U.S.

National statistics, 2006[1]	
Number of active-duty personnel	1.4 million
Number of married active-duty personnel	780,000 or more
Number of single parents who are in active duty	100,000
Number of family members of active duty personnel	2 million
Number of family members who are children of active duty personnel	1.24 million
Minnesota statistics, December 2003[2]	
Number of spouses of active-duty personnel	833
Number of children of active-duty personnel	1,751
Number of other dependents of active duty personnel	3

SOURCES: [1]Kozaryn, L. D. (2003). DoD studies mission: Family needs. *American Forces Press Service.* Retrieved September 14, 2006, from http://www.defenselink.mil
[2]USA4MilitaryFamilies.org, (2003). Active duty family members by state. Retrieved September 19, 2006, from http://usa4militaryfamilies.dod.mil

Marriage and the military

"In addition to the growing presence of women in the military, the occurrence of marriage among Servicemembers has also increased. However, unlike the growing percentages of women, the rise in marriage among Servicemembers has not maintained a steady growth. In FY 1973, approximately 40 percent of enlisted members were married. That statistic hit its high point in 1994 at 57 percent married, but decreased steadily to the FY 2003 rate of 49 percent. In FY 2004, nearly 50 percent of Active Component enlisted members were married. In fact, the proportion of married Servicemembers in FY 2004 is virtually identical to the proportion in 1977. Nevertheless, in FY 2004 approximately half of all soldiers, sailors, marines, and airmen are married, an increase of approximately 10 percentage points since the early 1970s.

"Newcomers to the military are less likely than their civilian age counterparts to be married. Similarly, military members tend to be less likely to be married than those in the civilian sector; however, the difference is much less pronounced in the total active force than it is with accessions. Among enlisted members, 50 percent of those on active duty and 47 percent in the Reserve Components were married as of the end of FY 2004. In the military, men were more likely to be married than women.

Minnesota's active duty military fathers

According to the Minnesota State Demographer's Office, "Minnesota does not have very many 'current' residents who are members of the military since [the state does not] have large military bases." Furthermore, "if the father is absent since he is in active duty, information on the household does not include him since he is not there." Therefore, Minnesota's active duty fathers are left uncounted, or counted as absent, if their service requires them to be housed outside of the state.

SOURCE: Gillaspy, T. (personal communication, September 19, 2006). Minnesota's active military fathers. Message sent to lorenn@albanytel.com, archived at lorenn@albanytel.com

"As one might expect, owing to their being older and financially more secure on average, officers were more likely to be married (68 percent of the Active Component and 73 percent of the Reserve Component officer corps were married) than enlisted personnel. Again, women officers were less likely than their male colleagues to be married.

SOURCE: Office of the Under Secretary of Defense, (2004). Population representation in the military servives 2004. Retrieved September 15, 2006 from Department of Defense: http://dod.mil

Barriers to father involvement

Frequency of child maltreatment

In cases where child maltreatment has been reported, mothers were perpetrators (without fathers) in 47.1% of all cases. Cases where fathers were involved (without mothers) totaled 19.9% of all cases. Mothers and fathers were mutually involved in maltreatment in 16.9% of all reported cases of child maltreatment. Fig. 6.2 does not show 16.1% of all cases of child maltreatment where neither parent was involved.[5]

These figures demonstrate that mothers overall have a higher incidence of engaging in child maltreatment. However, the statistics do not demonstrate a higher probability of maltreatment per hour of parent-child contact. In many households, mothers spend more time with their children; mothers are more likely than fathers to be single parents; and mothers are more likely to be the primary caretaker.

According to the U.S. Office on Child Abuse and Neglect, "Fathers who nurture and take significant responsibility for basic childcare for their children from an early age are significantly less likely to sexually abuse their children [in comparison to other fathers]. These fathers typically develop such a strong connection with their children that it decreases the likelihood of any maltreatment." Furthermore, father involvement "in the life of a family is also associated with lower levels of child neglect, even in families that may be facing other factors, such as unemployment and poverty." Without the moderating factor of positive family involvement, poverty and unemployment or underemployment "can increase a father's stress level, which may make him more likely to abuse his children physically." Additional aggravating factors for fathers who engage in child maltreatment include substance abuse, having been abused as a child, having witnessed domestic abuse as a child, or low self-worth and psychological distress.

Notably, children who live in father-absent homes "often face higher risks of physical abuse, sexual abuse, and neglect than children who live with their fathers".[5]

SOURCES: Citations for this page are listed on page 39.

Figure 6.2 **Reported perpetrators of child maltreatment**[5], U.S., 2003, percent of cases where mothers or fathers were involved, based on the 83.9 percent of all maltreatment cases where a parent was involved

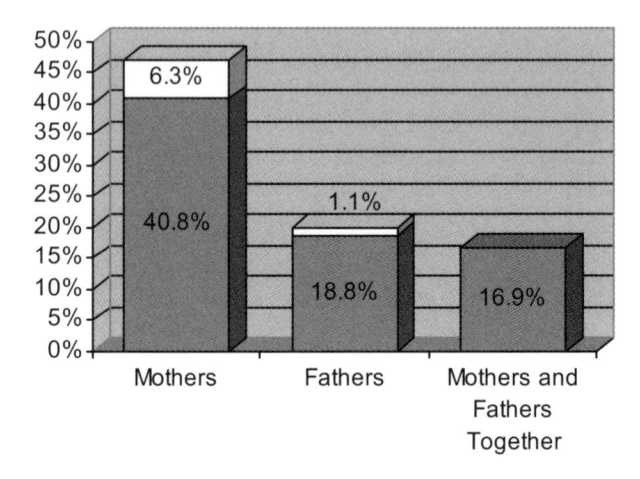

Category	Parent(s) alone	Parent(s) with another person
Mothers	40.8%	6.3%
Fathers	18.8%	1.1%
Mothers and Fathers Together	16.9%	

Child maltreatment statistics, Minnesota, 2004[6]

In 2004, almost 7,800 children were abused and neglected; 39 children suffered life-threatening injuries and 11 children died from maltreatment. Of these abused and neglected children:

- Most victims were younger than 6 years old.
- Boys were maltreatment victims more often than girls from age 1 to 10 years; girls suffered maltreatment more often than boys from age 11 through 17 years.
- Caucasian children accounted for 52 percent of maltreatment victims; Black children, 25 percent; American Indian children, 7 percent; Asian and Pacific Islander children, 3 percent. Children identified with two or more races accounted for 7 percent. Of all victims, 9 percent indicated Hispanic ethnicity.
- Seventy-three percent of all offenders were victims' birth parents. Other relatives, including stepparents, adoptive parents, grandparents and siblings accounted for 15 percent of offenders. Parents' companions accounted for 8 percent of offenders.

Barriers to father involvement

Prevalence of domestic violence

Overall, violent crime by intimate partners decreased by 9 percent between 2001 and 2004. Order for protection filings in Minnesota were highest at 14,172 in 1996 and decreased to 12,376 in 2004. Orders for protection are civil court orders which are granted to protect individuals from domestic violence.[3]

In 2001, reported cases of intimate partner violence[1]:
- 588,490 women were victims (approximately 85 percent of all reported victims)
- 103,220 men were victims (approximately 15 percent of all reported victims)

"In a national survey of more than 6,000 American families, 50 percent of the men who frequently assaulted their wives also frequently abused their children." The study also found that "the rate of child abuse by those [mothers] who have been beaten is at least double that of mothers whose husbands did not assault them." [2]

Violence and sexual abuse: Student reports of parental/adult abuse

According to the 2004 Minnesota Student Survey, 7% - 14% of students reported having been hit so hard by an adult in their households that they had marks or were afraid of the person who hit them. The statistics do not identify the gender of the adult offender, nor do the survey results indicate the specific relationship beyond "any adult in your household." Male 9th and 12th graders reported the lowest level of abuse (7%) while male 6th graders and female 9th graders reported the highest level (14%).[4]

A separate question on the student survey asked, "Has any older/stronger member of your family touched you sexually or had you touch them sexually?" Again, student responses vary based on age and gender. Male sixth graders answered yes 1% of the time while female 9th and 12th graders answered yes 4% of the time. Again, the survey does not report gender or relationship of the offender.[4]

> **The Best Part of Being a Dad**
>
> "Re-experiencing the world through your children's eyes. Seeing them experience things for the first time."
>
> - from a father who completed the Father Involvement Survey, child's age 0-4 years

SOURCES:
[1] U.S. Bureau of Justice Statistics. (2003). Crime Data Brief, Intimate Partner Violence, 1992-2001, in *The Facts on Domestic Violence*. San Francisco: Family Violence Prevention Fund. http://www.endabuse.org
[2] Strauss, Murray A., Gelles, Richard J. and Smith, Christine. (1990). Physical Violence in American Families; Risk Factors and Adaptations to Violence in 8,145 Families. New Brunswick: Transaction Publishers in *The facts on domestic violence*. San Francisco: Family Violence Prevention Fund. http://www.endabuse.org
[3] Minnesota Department of Public Safety, Office of Justice Programs. (2006). *OJP Fact Sheet: Domestic Violence*. St. Paul: Minnesota Department of Public Safety.
[4] Minnesota Student Survey Interagency Team. (2004). *2004 Minnesota Student Survey: County Tables* (Minnesota Center for Health Statistics). annkinney@state.mn.us.
[5] Rosenberg, J. & Wilcox, W.B. (2006). *The importance of fathers in the healthy development of children*. Washington DC: U.S. Office on Child Abuse and Neglect.
[6] Prevent Child Abuse Minnesota. (n.d.). *Child abuse prevention materials*. Retrieved August 12, 2006, from http://www.pcamn.org

Barriers to father involvement

Child welfare and kinship support

The Minnesota Department of Human Services promotes child welfare through in-home or out-of-home placements in order to achieve three primary outcomes: to protect children from abuse and neglect; to provide for a level of permanency and stability in the child's living situation; and to enhance the well-being of the children and their families.

"Of the 7,338 children in out-of-home care on Sept. 30, 2003, 20% were living with relatives while in care."[2] Relative searches were conducted for maternal relatives in 69% of applicable cases and for paternal relatives in 62% of cases.[1] "Of all Minnesota children in kinship care on September 30, 2003, 41.4% were White, 27% were Black, 5.4% were Hispanic, 16.5% were American Indian/Alaskan Native, and 9.6% were other races."[2]

According to a report issued by the Urban Institute, child welfare caseworkers knew the identity of 88% of nonresident fathers while 37% of fathers had not established paternity. In Minnesota, paternity was determined through having the father's name on the birth certificate in 26 percent of cases. Nine percent of fathers engaged in child welfare cases in Minnesota had relinquished their parental rights while 37 percent had their parental rights terminated. These figures for relinquishment and termination of parental rights in Minnesota were higher than in any of the other states included in the study.[3]

Figure 6.3 **Child welfare cases: Parent involvement in case planning**, mothers vs. fathers, Minnesota[1]

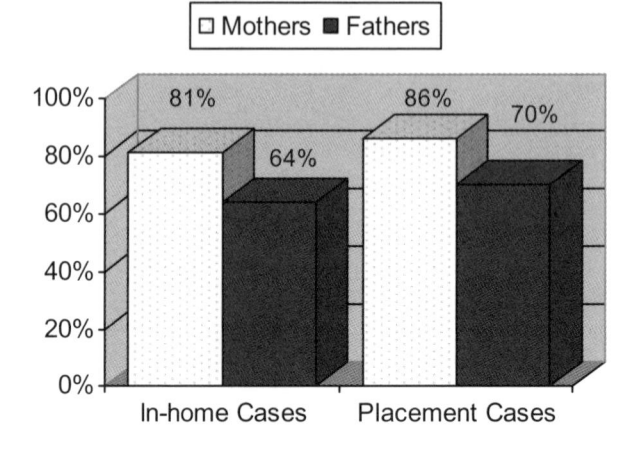

- In-home Cases: Mothers 81%, Fathers 64%
- Placement Cases: Mothers 86%, Fathers 70%

Figure 6.4 **Child welfare cases: Parent involvement in case planning**, mothers vs. fathers, Minnesota vs. U.S.

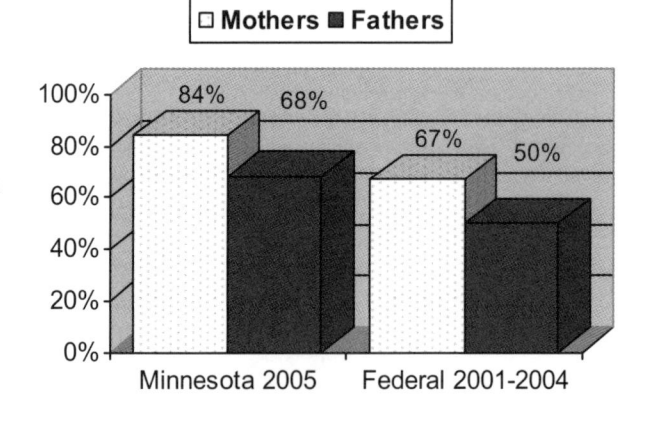

- Minnesota 2005: Mothers 84%, Fathers 68%
- Federal 2001-2004: Mothers 67%, Fathers 50%

SOURCES: [1]Minnesota Department of Human Services. (2005). *2005 Minnesota Child and Family Service Reviews* (Quarterly Supervisor's Forum: Engaging and Involving Fathers). Retrieved March 1, 2006, from http://www.dhs.state.mn.us. Also includes related data from "Minnesota Child and Family Service Reviews: Fathers Report: January—December 2005.
[2] Child Welfare League of America. (2006). *Minnesota's Children 2006*. Retrieved July 20, 2006 from http://www.cwla.org/advoacy/statefactsheets/2006minnesota.htm
[3] Urban Institute. (2006 April). *What about the dads? Child welfare agencies efforts to identify, locate, and involve nonresident fathers.* Washington,DC: Urban Institute.

Barriers to father involvement

Figure 6.5 **Frequency of parent / child visits for families engaged in child welfare cases**, Minnesota[1]

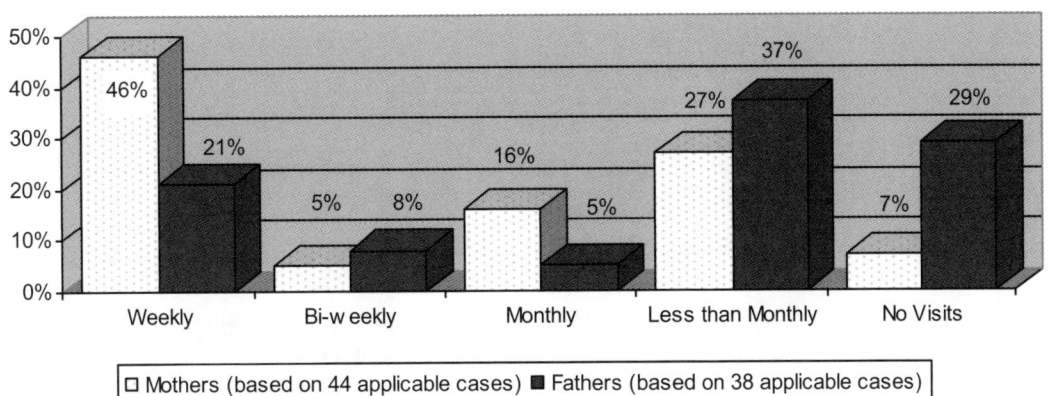

	Weekly	Bi-weekly	Monthly	Less than Monthly	No Visits
Mothers	46%	5%	16%	27%	7%
Fathers	21%	8%	5%	37%	29%

☐ Mothers (based on 44 applicable cases) ■ Fathers (based on 38 applicable cases)

Figure 6.6 **Child welfare cases: Efforts made to promote and maintain the parent / child relationship**, Minnesota, mothers vs. fathers[1]

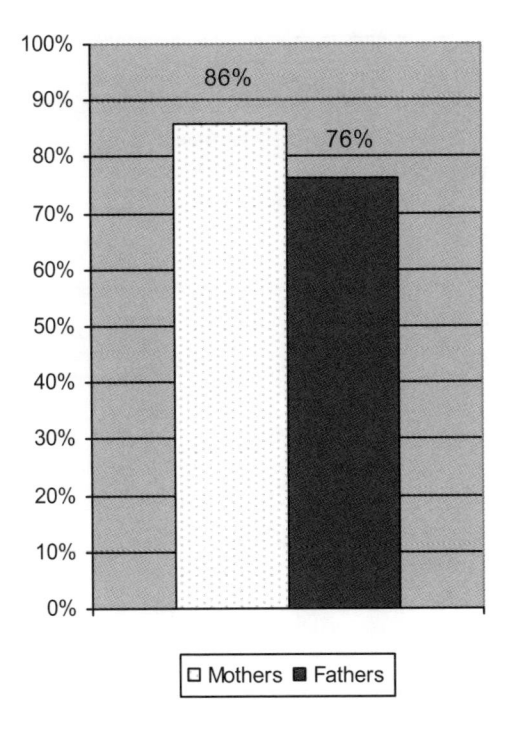

- Mothers: 86%
- Fathers: 76%

Nonresident father engagement

"Caseworkers report telling almost all contacted fathers about the child's out-of-home placement (96%) and sharing the case plan with them (94%). Half of the contacted fathers expressed an interest in having the child live with them. Caseworkers reported considering placement with 45 percent of contacted fathers, ranging from 34 percent in Massachusetts to 51 percent in Minnesota." Paternal relatives were considered as placement options 67 percent of the time in Minnesota (54 percent average across the study states).[3]

Nonresident father visitation

The Urban Institute found that, among nonresident fathers, a high percentage fail to attend all of their planned visits with their child(ren). The study found that over 40% of fathers do attend all or most of planned visits. However, nearly 28% only sometimes or rarely attend. Additionally, more than one-quarter (28.5%) never attend or have no planned visits.[3]

SOURCES: Identified on page 40.

Barriers to father involvement

Figure 6.7 **Identifying nonresident fathers**, Who was asked to identify the father?[3]

Percent asked:

Child's mother	83.7%
Mother's relatives	44.4%
Another worker	39.7%
Child (only asked on children over 6)	37.9%
Child's sibling	10.8%
Father's relatives	9.6%
Other	18.5%

Percent who provided information (of those asked):

Child's mother	30.9%
Mother's relatives	20.9%
Another worker	30.4%
Child (only asked on children over 6)	23.4%
Child's sibling	21.1%
Father's relatives	38.2%
Other	23.2%

SOURCE: Identified on page 40.

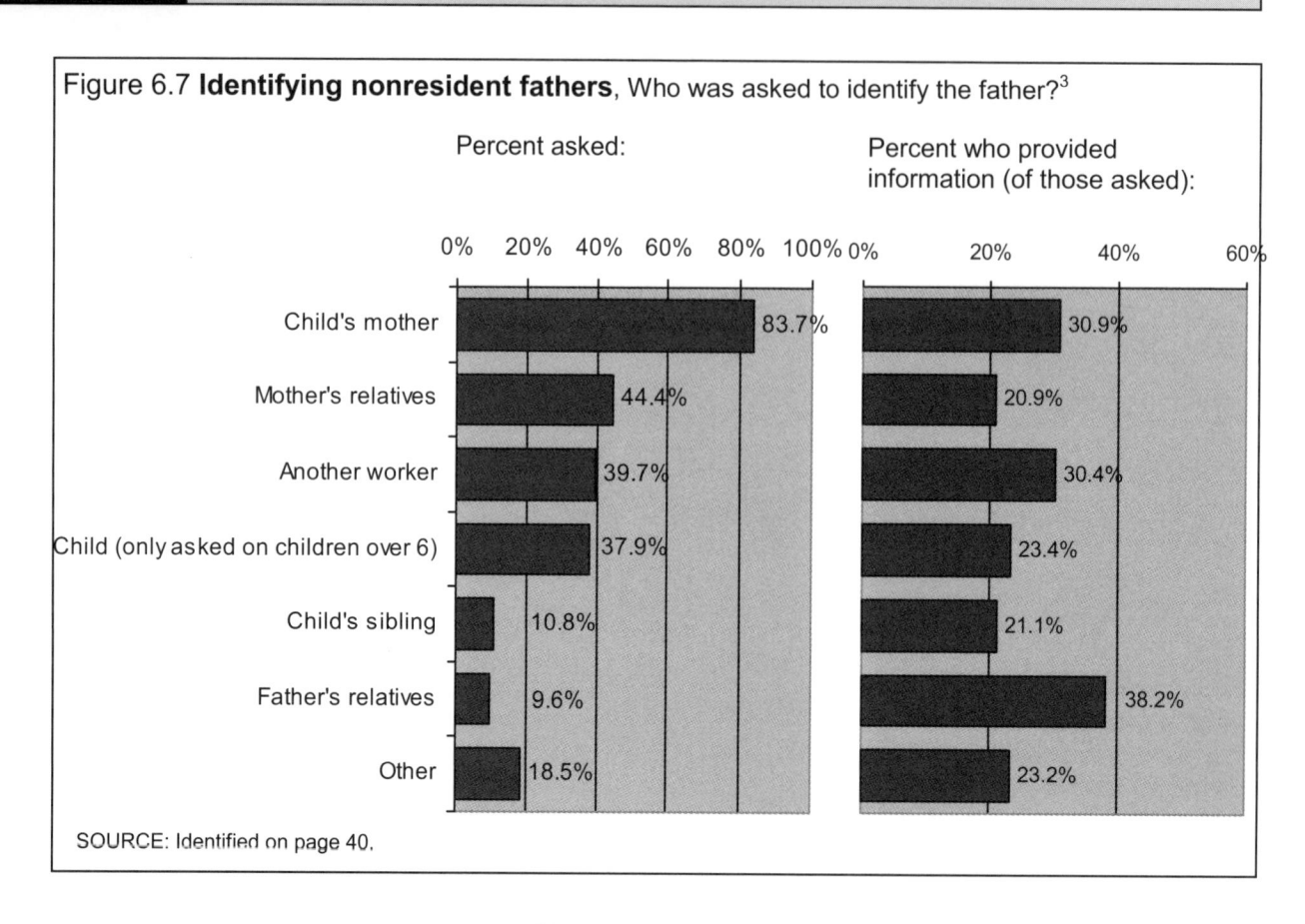

Children who have met their nonresident fathers

Figure 6.8 demonstrates that, among children who live without their biological fathers, Black children are far more likely to know their fathers. Among children who do not live with their fathers, only 6% of Black children have never seen their father compared to 25% of Asian children, 21% of Hispanic children, and 18% of White children.

These statistics support the notion of "social fatherhood" in the African American community, as discussed in Chapter 7, page 46.

Figure 6.8 **Percentage of children with no biological father in their home who have never seen their father**, by race/ethnicity, 2001, U.S.

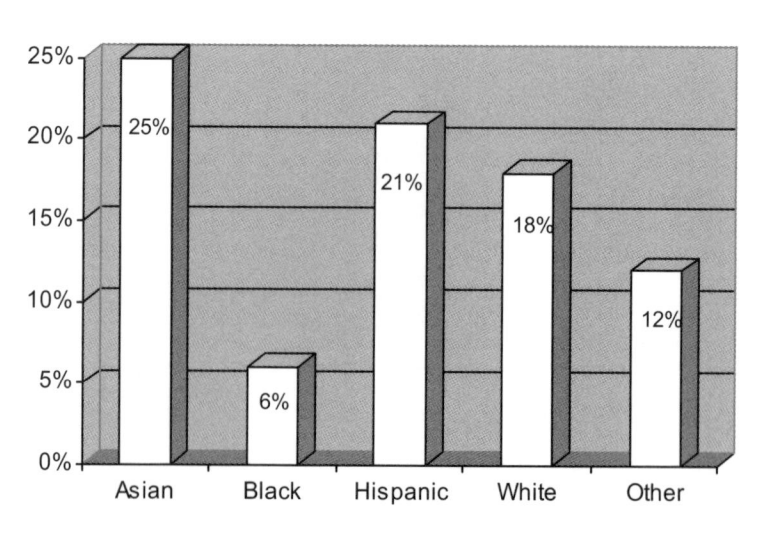

Race/Ethnicity	Percentage
Asian	25%
Black	6%
Hispanic	21%
White	18%
Other	12%

SOURCE: Avenilla, F., Rosenthal, E., and Tice, P. (2006). *Fathers of U.S. children born in 2001: Findings from the early childhood longitudinal study, birth cohort* (NCES 2006-002). U.S. Department of Education, National Center for Education Statistics. Washington, DC: U.S. Government Printing Office.

Special populations of Minnesota's fathers

Chapter 7

The previous chapter discusses unique circumstances which create challenges or barriers that nearly any father could face at some point in his life. This chapter explores specific populations of fathers who live outside of the majority of two-parent married households.

Each of these populations brings unique attributes and special challenges to the role of father. The men in this chapter are among the groups of fathers that were most difficult to locate for this report. Although uncounted and/or discounted in many ways, these groups of men are important to consider in order to see the full picture of fatherhood in Minnesota.

Low-income young fathers: Based on a study of teen mothers in Minnesota

"Of all births in the United States in 1998, 4.6 percent were to teens under age 18 and 7.9 percent to teens age 18 and 19. The births to teens under age 18 made up 2.7 percent of all births in Minnesota."

The Minnesota Family Investment Program (MFIP — Minnesota's welfare program) conducted a longitudinal study of new applicants who were teen mothers at baseline; all information in this section is derived from the study report, published in 2003. According to the report, "Many of the teen mothers...grew up under difficult circumstances. Forty-five percent remembered their family receiving welfare when they themselves were children." Thirty eight percent of their fathers were involved in crime, violence, or chemical dependency. Only one in three came from a home with both parents present for most of their childhood.

"Only 16 of the 248 teen mothers ever married the father of their firstborn child and 207 had never been married by 30 months after the MFIP application. Much speculation has centered on the marriageability of the males teen mothers know and on the mothers' self-esteem and own presumed marriageability. The participants themselves spoke about problems in the fathers' lives...and the teens' own independence as single parents as factors in their not marrying."

After 30 months only 9 were still married to the father while 18 percent were living with the father without marriage.

Table 7.1 **Fathers' statistics: Fathers of teen mothers' firstborn children**, Minnesota*

Average age at child's birth	20.6 years
Known high school graduate	42%
Employed at time of baby's birth	50%
Established paternity	73%
Married the mother of the child (before or after the child's birth)	6%
History of substance abuse, violence, or crime	59%

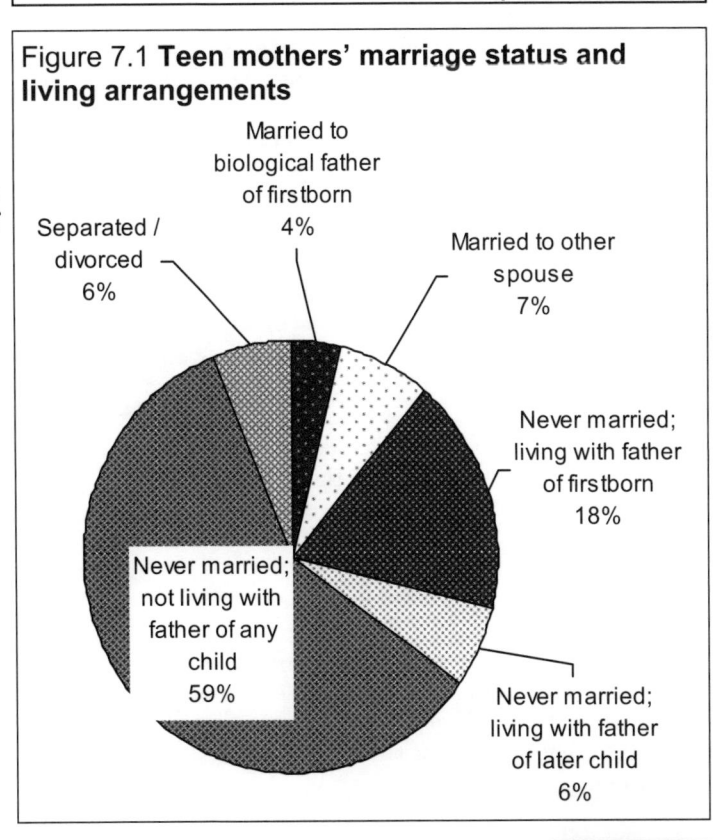

Figure 7.1 **Teen mothers' marriage status and living arrangements**

- Married to biological father of firstborn: 4%
- Married to other spouse: 7%
- Separated / divorced: 6%
- Never married; living with father of firstborn: 18%
- Never married; not living with father of any child: 59%
- Never married; living with father of later child: 6%

page 43

Special populations of Minnesota's fathers

Barriers for teen fathers:
"The biological fathers of the teens' first children had numerous barriers to successful parenting and economic stability. According to the teen mothers, 59 percent of these fathers had experienced problems with substance abuse, violence, or crime. Forty percent had been involved in criminal activities. Twenty-five percent of the fathers were five or more years older than the mothers, including 5 percent who were more than 10 years older. Half of the fathers were unemployed when the baby was born. At month 30, 46 percent were known to be working, 24 percent were unemployed. Less than half were known to be high school graduates at the time of the baby's birth. Paternity had not been established for 27 percent of the firstborn children, and 80 percent of the fathers not in the household 30 months after MFIP application paid no child support. Twenty-three percent of fathers had no contact with the child for at least a year.

Involving teen fathers:
The report asks the following questions:
- What is the right mix of enforcement of child support obligations and outreach to engage fathers in the lives of their children?
- What social and employment supports might help low-income men improve their earnings and nurture their children?
- How can fathers be helped in dealing with issues like chemical dependency, violence, and crime to be better equipped to be good fathers?

Teen mothers' relationship with their own parents:
"Altogether 88 percent of the teen mothers lived with their mothers during most of their childhood and 50 percent lived with their father during that time. A third (34 percent) were raised in two-parent families by their own mother and father." Four percent lived only or primarily with their father.

"More of the teen mothers were closer to their own mothers than to their fathers. Most characterized as mostly good their childhood relationships with their mothers (75%) and with their fathers (63%). These approvals were over 80 percent for both parents if the teens had lived with them."

The teen mothers reported that the person who was most supportive during their own childhood was their mother (57%); their father (7%); both mother and father equally (10%).

SOURCE: Minnesota Department of Human Services. (2005). *Minnesota family investment program longitudinal study: four years after baseline.* St. Paul: Author.

* Based on the responses of the 248 teen mothers who completed the MFIP Longitudinal Study.

** Two and a half years (30 months) after the mothers' initial survey.

Figure 7.2 **Father of firstborn child to teen mother: Father's contact with child after two and a half years****

- Living with child 19%
- No contact for at least a year 24%
- Contact several times each week 16%
- Contact less than once a month 22%
- Contact one to four times per month 19%

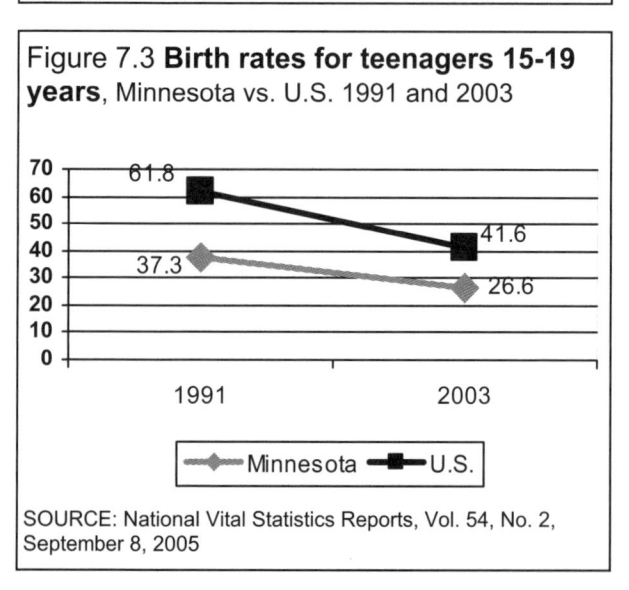

Figure 7.3 **Birth rates for teenagers 15-19 years**, Minnesota vs. U.S. 1991 and 2003

	1991	2003
Minnesota	37.3	26.6
U.S.	61.8	41.6

SOURCE: National Vital Statistics Reports, Vol. 54, No. 2, September 8, 2005

Special populations of Minnesota's fathers

Grandparents raising grandchildren

In Minnesota in 2006, 33,975 children (or 2.6%) lived in grandparent-headed households.[3]

Meanwhile, in 2004, approximately 17,852 Minnesota grandparents had primary responsibility for their grandchildren.[2]

"The phenomenon of grandparents caring for their grandchildren isn't new, and can be found in all socioeconomic, ethnic and religious groups. There are a variety of problems that can prevent parents from caring for their child: incarceration, drug or alcohol abuse, physical or mental illness, serving in the military, unplanned pregnancies, financial difficulties — even untimely deaths."[3]

Grandparents caring for their grandchildren can be temporary—such as when a parent is ill or in some kind of trouble—or it can be permanent involving legal guardianship and adoption.[3]

The poverty rate of grandparents living with their grandchildren tends to be considerably lower than poverty rates among single custodial mothers or fathers.[2]

Table 7.2 **Grandparents in Minnesota,** living with own grandchildren under 18 years, in households[1]

Total number	52,952
Number responsible for grandchildren (i.e., do not live with the parents of the grandchildren)	17,852
Grandfathers	36%
Married	71%
In labor force	76%
In poverty	8%

Family, friend and neighbor caregivers[4]

According to a 2004 Minnesota statewide household child care survey, "Relatives, primarily grandmothers, outnumber non-relative caregivers." The report notes that 52% of family, friend and neighbor (FFN) caregivers are the child's grandparent, including 8 percent who are grandfathers.

This data set differs from "grandparents raising grandchildren." The FFN caregiver grandparents are more likely to provide support to the grandchildren's parents by babysitting or providing day care services.

The report also finds that most family, friend and neighbor caregivers are females (86%), and just 14% are males. In the Twin Cities metro area, families are more likely than Greater Minnesota families to rely on a caregiver from within their ethnic community for encouragement and support.

Few FFN caregivers report significant problems when providing child care. According to the report, "the most commonly reported problems include "not having enough time for him or herself" (30 percent), "being comfortable with disciplining other people's children" (23 percent), "having to constantly change plans or routines" (21 percent) and "long or irregular hours" (18.5 percent). The report does not break out results by gender of the caregiver.

SOURCES: [1]U.S. Census Bureau. *American factfinder, Minnesota selected social characteristics: 2004.* [Data Set: 2004 American Community Survey].
[2] Child Welfare League of America. (2006). *Minnesota's Children 2006.* Retrieved July 20, 2006 from http://www.cwla.org/advoacy/statefactsheets/2006minnesota.htm
[3]Remington, M. R. (October-December, 2006). Second time around: Grandparents raising children. *Family Times.*
[4]Chase, R., Arnold, J., Schauben, L., and Shardlow, B. (February 2006). *Family Friend and Neighbor Caregivers: Results of the 2004 Minnesota statewide household child care survey.* St. Paul: Wilder Research.

Special populations of Minnesota's fathers

Table 7.3 **Same-sex male partner households**, Minnesota, 2000

• Same-sex unmarried partner households, male partners	4,290 couples
• Same-sex unmarried partner households, male partners, living with their own and/or unrelated children*	17.9% have children
• Approximate number of households with male partners, living with their own and/or unrelated children*	768 families have children

Although the U.S. Census does not count the number of gay fathers, it does attempt to count the number of unmarried same-sex partners who have children under 18 years of age living in the household.

SOURCE: U.S. Census Bureau. (2003). *Married couple and unmarried-partner households:2000* (cnsr-5). Washington DC: Simmons, T. & O'Connell, M.
*In this report, "own child" refers to the son/daughter of the householder. This includes any child under the age of 18 who is a biological, adopted, or stepchild of the householder.

The challenge of counting gay fathers

It should be noted that, to comply with the 1996 Federal Defense of Marriage Act, the Census Bureau invalidated any year 2000 census responses of "same-sex spouse" and allocated those responses as "unmarried partner". Due to court challenges to the legality of same sex marriages, federal limitations, and inconsistent data processing between the 1990 and 2000 census reports, "direct comparison of the 1990 and 2000 estimates is not substantively valid."

Adding to the challenge of counting gay fathers is the fact that the census does not take sexual orientation into account. Therefore, it is quite likely that the figures fail to account for gay single fathers or gay fathers who live with adult females.

SOURCE: U.S. Census Bureau. (n.d.). *Technical note on same-sex unmarried partners.* Retrieved October 10, 2006, from http://www.census.gov/population/www/cen2000/samesex.html

> **Most Challenging Part of Fathering**
>
> "having enough energy to keep up with my child"
>
> - from a father who completed the Father Involvement Survey, child's age 0-4 years

Social fathers

According to the book, *Black fathers: An invisible presence in America*, "African American boys and young men with and without resident biological fathers in the home tend to seek out social fathers in the extended family and surrounding Black community to augment or fulfill the fathering role." Social fatherhood includes "men who assume some or all of the roles fathers are expected to perform in a child's life, whether or not they are biological fathers. [Social fatherhood] extends to men...who provide a significant degree of nurturance, moral and ethical guidance, companionship, emotional support, and financial responsibility in the lives of children."

The importance of social fathers was highlighted in a 2002 report about Hennepin County's African American Men Project. The report, "Crossroads: Choosing a New Direction", recommended that public policy should recognize the importance of fathers in the family, as opposed to focusing only on mothers and children. The document went on to say, "This should include widening our focus to include males across the lifespan who play (or could potentially play) significant roles in the lives of families."

Fathers' physical and mental health — Chapter 8

This chapter explores the health of Minnesota's fathers. An understanding of the physical and mental well-being of men in families is vital in order to begin to determine fathers' abilities to adequately support their children in healthy ways.

As noted later in this report (see Recommendations, Chapter 11), some chapters were easier than others to fill with pertinent data about Minnesota's fathers. In various sections, including this section about health, extensive data was either non-existent, outdated, incomplete, or unavailable.

Figure 8.1 **Health status of fathers**, Minnesota vs. U.S., based on percentage of children with biological, step, foster, and adoptive fathers living in household with children / youth (ages 0-17)

Respondents answered the question, "Would you say that in general (child's father's) health is excellent, very good, good, fair, or poor?" Percent of children ages 0-17 living with fathers whose health status is excellent to poor.

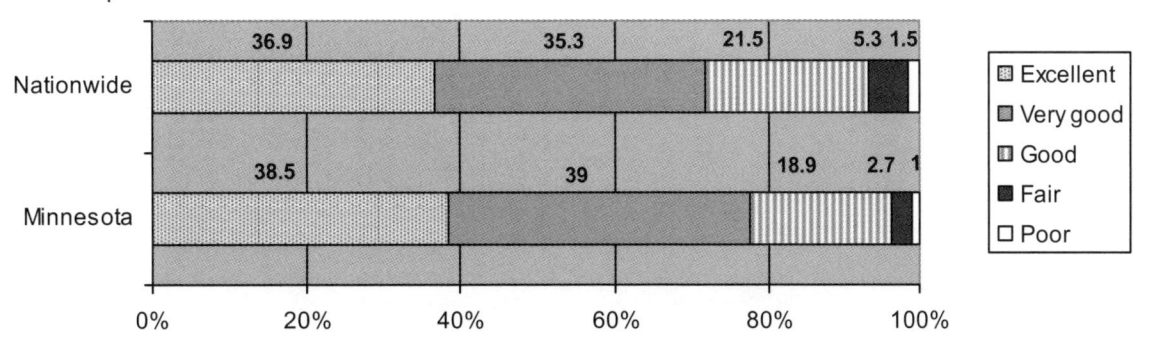

	Excellent	Very good	Good	Fair	Poor
Nationwide	36.9	35.3	21.5	5.3	1.5
Minnesota	38.5	39	18.9	2.7	1

Figure 8.2 **Mental health status of fathers**, Minnesota vs. U.S., based on percentage of children with biological, step, foster, and adoptive fathers living in household with children / youth (ages 0-17)

Respondents answered the question, "Would you say that in general (child's father's) mental and emotional health is excellent, very good, good, fair, or poor?" Percent of children ages 0-17 living with fathers whose mental health status is excellent to poor.

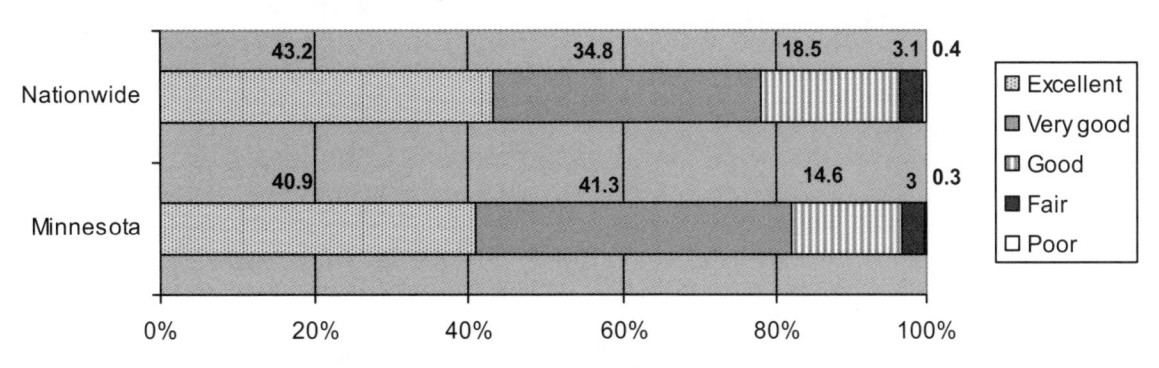

	Excellent	Very good	Good	Fair	Poor
Nationwide	43.2	34.8	18.5	3.1	0.4
Minnesota	40.9	41.3	14.6	3	0.3

SOURCE: National Survey of Children's Health. (2005). *Child and adolescent health measurement initiative.* Retrieved July 10, 2006 from http://www.nschdata.org/content/ChartbooksPubsAndPresentations.aspx

Fathers' physical and mental health

Fathers' health and suicide

Considerable data sources show that men are at a significantly higher risk of death by suicide than women, as shown in Figure 8.3. Rates are higher among males in certain demographic groups including: men over 65 years of age, adolescents / young adults, White or American Indian men, and others. Across the nation, individuals in Western states are more likely to commit suicide; spring is the time of year with the highest incidence of suicide. Lower rates of suicide occur in Midwestern and Northeastern states and during the winter. Additionally, individuals experiencing family violence, sexual abuse, domestic abuse, incarceration, depression, or mental disorders are at increased risk.

The impact that fathers can have on their own children's lives is well-documented. "Fatherless children are at dramatically greater risk of suicide." According to some sources, children raised without fathers or in single-parent homes comprise approximately 75% of all adolescent suicides. However, data is difficult to find which shows whether fatherhood has any impact on a man's own risk of dying by suicide. Rates of suicide among married men are lower than among divorced or widowed men.

SOURCES: U.S. Department of Health and Human Services, National Center for Health Statistics. (1993). *Survey on Child Health*. Washington, D.C.: Author.

National Center for Injury Prevention and Control, U.S. Centers for Disease Control and Prevention. (September 2006). *Suicide: Fact Sheet*. Retrieved November 12, 2006 from www.cdc.gov/ncipc/factsheets/suifacts.htm

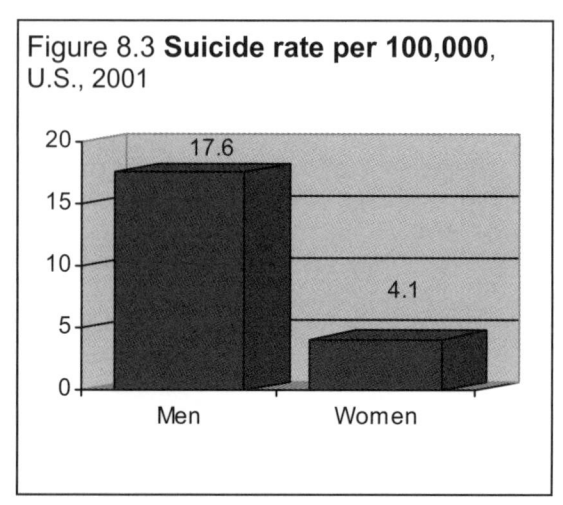

Figure 8.3 **Suicide rate per 100,000**, U.S., 2001

- Men: 17.6
- Women: 4.1

SOURCE: National Institute of Mental Health, National Institutes of Health, 2003

Parents' mental health and marriage

"Researchers looked at data on a group of almost 5,000 births (both marital and non-marital) in major U.S. cities. The data included interviews with mothers and fathers, as well as assessments of anxiety, depression, heavy drinking, illicit drug use, incarceration and domestic abuse.

"In general, unmarried parents reported more mental-health and behavioral problems than married parents.

"But there were considerable differences within the group of single parents. For instance, single parents whose relationships ended before the birth of the child reported more problems than other unmarried parents. And parents who were currently not cohabiting or romantically involved reported the most mental-health problems.

"Unmarried fathers who lived with their partners were more than twice as likely than married fathers to have been in jail; nonromantic fathers were more than three times as likely as married fathers to have been in jail. Unmarried fathers who were still romantically linked to the mother of their child were more likely to have experienced a major episode of depression compared to married fathers. Unmarried, nonromantic dads experienced the highest rates of depression and anxiety, the study found. Nonromantic fathers were the most likely to have been violent, and married fathers the least likely. Partner violence was twice as high among romantically linked but unmarried couples as among married couples."

SOURCE: American Journal of Public Health. (2006). Marriage boosts parents' mental health [Electronic version]. *Forbes Magazine*. Online, September 28, 2006.

section two

Filling the Gaps

Surveys to broaden our base of understanding

Father-child involvement — Chapter 9

This chapter brings together national and statewide data that describes how fathers are spending time with their children. This has been an important area of research about fathers since the 1970s. It is also an area of some controversy about how to define and measure father involvement (Palkovitz, 1997). Past research has often focused on the comparison of the level of father involvement to mother involvement. The planning committee for this report recommended that information on types of father involvement and level of father involvement would be an important area to include in the final document.

A decision was made to conduct a survey of fathers in Minnesota to assess the current level of father involvement. During the fall of 2006, **567 fathers completed the Minnesota Father Involvement Survey**. The survey included two versions: one for fathers of younger children 0—4 years old and a separate version for fathers with children 5—12 years of age. When appropriate, results are shown for the two groups of fathers.

Chapter 9 is divided into five parts:
- Part A: Attitudes about fatherhood and level of involvement in parenting activities
- Part B: The best and most challenging parts of fatherhood and who fathers turn to when they have concerns about parenting
- Part C: Demographic characteristics of the sample population and comparisons to the general population of fathers in Minnesota
- Part D: Comparisons with relevant state and national data sources, when available
- Part E: Survey Methodology

The survey of father involvement provides valuable information about fathers of children 0-13 in Minnesota. Fathers clearly value the multiple roles that they play. They are very involved with their young children in regular caretaking activities and continue a high level of involvement with older children. They describe joys as well as challenges around raising children. Most men appear to look to family members and friends for information and support for parenting. A number of fathers are also involved in parenting education and support programs and report them as an important source of information.

Part A: Attitudes about fatherhood and level of involvement in parenting activities

Table 9.1 **Rating of fatherhood role activities: Survey respondents versus Early Childhood Longitudinal Study (ECLS)**

Father role	Survey respondents: Children's ages 0-4 % Very important	Survey respondents: Children's ages 5-12 % Very important	ECLS ranking [1]
Show love and affection	92	87	1
Safety/ Protection	89	88	2
Moral guidance	84	85	4
Take time to play	78	71	5
Teach and encourage	77	74	6
Financial care	76	70	3

This table is discussed on the following page.

[1] ECLS 2006 study. Fathers of U.S. children born in 2001

Father-child involvement

One of the questions in the survey asked fathers to rate the importance of different fatherhood role functions. As shown in Table 9.1 (previous page), fathers of the 0-4 year olds reported, 'showing love and affection' as the highest rated role with 'safety/ protection' as a close second. While all of the roles for this group were rated as important the lowest rated role was provider (financial care). The pattern for fathers of the older children (5-12 year olds) was similar with 'safety/ protection' at the top of the list and 'show love and affection' as a close second, while only 70% rated the provider role as very important. These results suggest a value shift in roles for fathers where the nurturer and protector role are valued above the provider role. This reflects a possible shift in values or perhaps may reflect that fathers in this group who are highly educated may feel the provider role has been met and they want to focus on the other roles of nurturer, protector, moral guide, playmate, and teacher. There are a few notable differences in ratings between the two groups of fathers that reflect the ages of the children. For example there is less emphasis on play and love & affection with the older children. The comparison group from the Early Childhood Longitudinal study shows a very similar ranking of roles with the exception of provider which was ranked as 3rd out of 6 roles. The ranking process was different in the two studies so the comparisons are limited.

Tables 9.2 and 9.3 summarize fathers' reports about their engagement on a variety of different activities with their children. Table 9.2 lists the caretaking activities in order of the percent of fathers who reported engaging in these activities with their children ages 0-4 every day to 1-2 times a week. Fathers who live with their children have regular opportunities to engage in

Table 9.2 **Father activities with children ages 0-4: Survey respondents versus ECLS**

Caretaking activities	Daily to 1 - 2 times a week	ECLS comparison[1]
Holds and comforts child	98%	99%
Play interactive games	96%	89%
Sets and Enforce rules	95%	NA
Change diaper/ toileting help	93%	87%
Helps get dressed	93%	81%
Takes child outside	93%	62%
Prepares food/ meals	92%	87%
Puts child to bed	90%	85%
Reads books	87%	72%
Takes child on errands	82%	90%
Sings songs	81%	89%
Washes/ bathes	80%	55%
Tells stories	72%	71%
Gets up during the night	63%	71%
Drops off at child care	47%	40%

[1]Children in ECLS average age was 9 months

Table 9.3 **Father activities with children 5-12**

	Daily to 1-2 times a week	Few times a month
Take child on errand	83%	16%
Help with homework	78%	11%
Read/look at books	73%	17%
Watch TV with child	73%	18%
Sports/active play	71%	20%
Household chores	71%	22%
Supervise play with friends	54%	31%
Attend religious service	50%	19%
Play board games	42%	40%
Help build/repair something	44%	36%
Take on special outing	36%	59%
Play computer/video game	36%	33%
Lead child in group activity	30%	16%

Father-child involvement

all of the activities listed except the final two items—gets up during the night and drops off at child care. By age 4 many children are sleeping through the night which explains the lower percentage of fathers reporting this activity. Dropping children off at day care also is only possible for dads whose children attend child care programs. The high level of involvement may be related to the high education level of this group of fathers and is consistent with the values expressed in the roles that fathers value. The comparison to fathers in the ECLS study demonstrates similar high levels of involvement mediated by the age of the children (average age 9 months). The age of the children in the ECLS study means that dads were less likely to take their babies outside, bathe them or read books to them. On the other hand, they were more likely to take their child on errands (probably with mom), sing songs and get up with their infants at night time.

Table 9.3 (previous page) summarizes the frequency that fathers of 5-12 year olds interact with their children on a regular, daily to weekly schedule versus a couple of times a month. The percentage of fathers who engage in regular activities is lower in this group. There are two reasons for this change in the level of interaction. First, this group of children is older and more independent and the activities listed are different in nature than the caretaking activities included in the list for children ages 0-4. The second reason for a lower level of shared father-child activities is that a higher percent of the fathers in this group reported being non-resident fathers and have limited opportunities for interaction. The activities toward the bottom of the list are also less frequent. Taking a child on an outing, playing video games, or building something together are less likely to occur on routine daily or weekly basis. The number of dads who lead a group at least 1-2 times a month (almost 50%) is very high considering the time and energy required to take on this task.

Table 9.4 reports on fathers' level of satisfaction with parenting. The fathers of the younger group report a very high level of satisfaction (92.6%). The fathers of the older group of children also report a high level of satisfaction (85.5%) but also a higher level of dissatisfaction. This can be related to the fathers in this group who may be divorced and not currently living with their children.

Table 9.5 describes fathers' self-ratings about their quality of fathering. A high percentage of all three groups describe themselves as better than average, 0-4= 87.2%, 5-12=82.8%, and 79% of the ECLS study fathers of infants rated themselves as better than average fathers.

Table 9.4 Fathers' satisfaction with parenting

Level of satisfaction	Child ages 0-4	Child ages 5-12
Very satisfied	52.0%	41.2%
Satisfied	40.6%	44.1%
Neither satisfied / dissatisfied	5.0%	9.8%
Dissatisfied	1.4%	3.3%
Very dissatisfied	1.4%	2.0%

Table 9.5 Fathers' self-rating of fathering quality

Self-rating	Child ages 0-4	ages 5-12	ECLS[1]
Very good father	45.6%	40.6%	49.0%
Better than average	41.6%	42.2%	30.0%
Average	11.4%	13.9%	17.0%
Having some trouble	1.4%	2.9%	2.0%
Not very good	0.0%	0.4%	0.5%

[1]ECLS study fathers of infants 2006

Father-child involvement

Part B: The best and most challenging parts of fatherhood and who fathers turn to when they have concerns about parenting

Figure 9.1 summarizes the main themes that were reported by fathers in both groups about the most rewarding part of being a dad. The dominant theme was watching the child grow, learn and develop for both groups. For the fathers of 5-12 year olds, the emphasis was on watching children's successes and witnessing their maturity. Another popular theme was feeling loved by the child. Dads in both groups reported enjoying the greetings, hugs, and kisses their children gave them. Fathers of older children enjoyed active play with their children, giving guidance, and being a role model. Fathers reported a variety of themes that are consistent with their roles as nurturer, moral guide, playmate and protector.

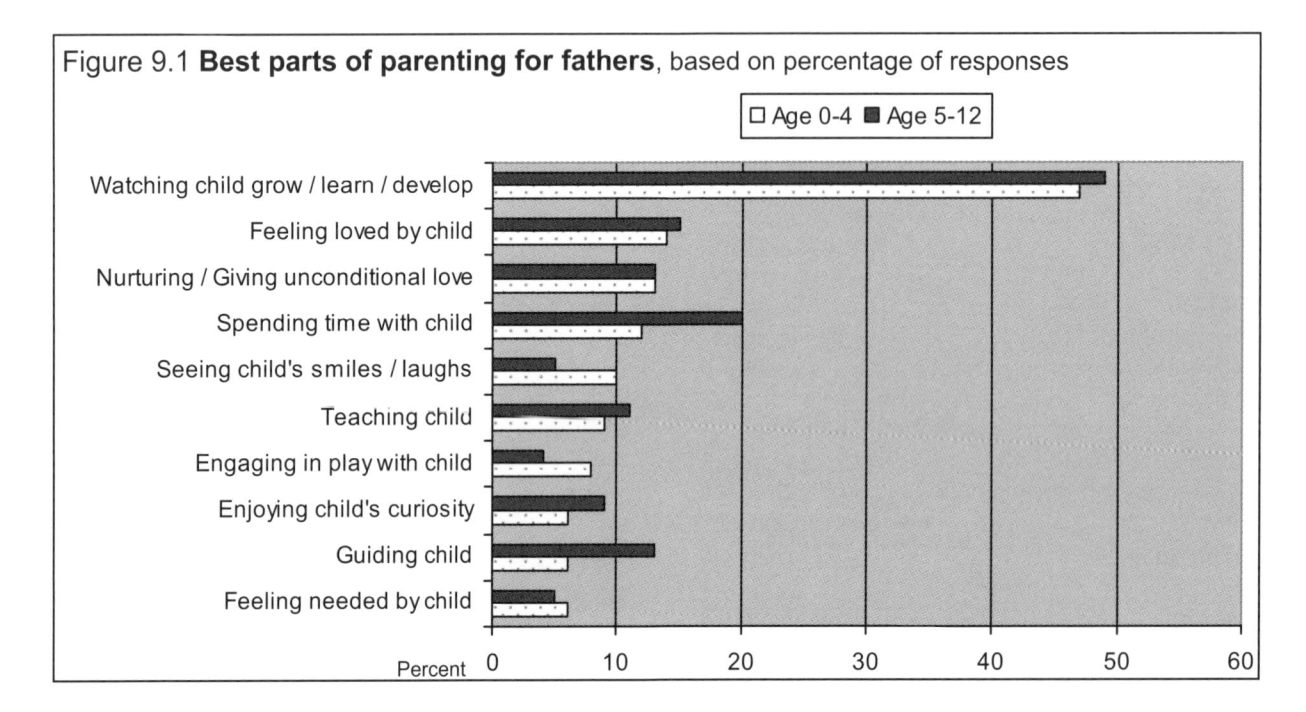

Figure 9.1 **Best parts of parenting for fathers**, based on percentage of responses

Figure 9.2 (following page) describes fathers' responses to the most challenging parts of fatherhood. The theme that was reported most frequently was discipline or setting limits. This was higher for fathers of young children where one of the tasks of parents is to develop a style of discipline. The issues around discipline for older children are different as fathers struggle with consistency at this stage. A second area mentioned by a number of fathers is staying calm and controlling their emotions. Lack of time was also a common theme that was expressed by both groups of fathers. Sometimes this was described as a lack of time with children, or too many things to do or a lack of time due to work demands. Conflict with the child's mother was also reported by a number of fathers. The fathers of 5-12 year olds were more likely to report issues related to conflicts around child visitation and child support. Fathers of the older group also were more concerned about teaching their child good morals and some described struggles with the feelings around lack of control they experienced as their children got older and were more independent. Fathers expressed a wide range of challenges which reflect the difficulties that most parents face. The fathers who expressed the most emotional concerns were divorced, non-residential fathers who were frustrated by the barriers they faced in trying to spend time with their children.

Father-child involvement

Figure 9.2 **Most challenging parts of fatherhood**, based on percentage of responses

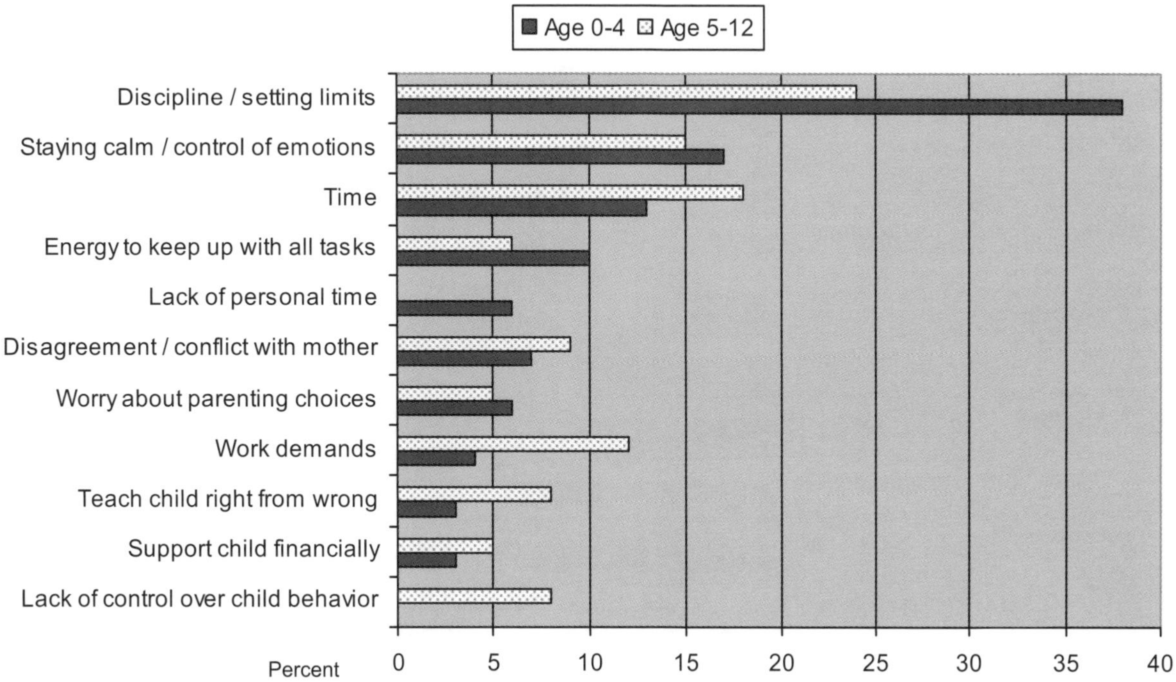

■ Age 0-4 ▨ Age 5-12

Category	Age 0-4	Age 5-12
Discipline / setting limits	38	24
Staying calm / control of emotions	17	15
Time	13	18
Energy to keep up with all tasks	10	6
Lack of personal time	6	—
Disagreement / conflict with mother	7	9
Worry about parenting choices	6	5
Work demands	4	12
Teach child right from wrong	3	8
Support child financially	3	5
Lack of control over child behavior	—	8

Percent

The final open-ended question in the survey asked fathers to list their main sources of support for parenting questions or concerns. Figure 9.3 (following page) summarizes the most frequently mentioned sources of support for fathers who participated in the survey. The general terms used to describe sources of support, "family and friends," often lacked specificity. Family might include a spouse, father, brother or in-law. Spouses/partners were the most frequently mentioned specific family members. Friends also were listed by a number of fathers in both groups and more frequently by fathers with older children. This term could be used to describe members in a parent group, neighbors, or peers at work so the term could encompass a number of people in some of the less frequently mentioned groups. It was interesting to note the high frequency of ECFE and father's programs as an important source of information. This reflects the MFFN network that was used to recruit fathers and serves as a potential source of bias. A number of fathers also used books and the Internet to help answer questions. A smaller number use health care providers, teachers, and religion as important sources of parenting information. Two other responses that are noteworthy are the low number of co-workers that were listed and the number of men who reported that they either had no sources for information or support or depended only upon themselves. Many of the participants also listed more than one possible source of information and support.

> **The Best Part of Being a Dad**
>
> "cuddling up at night after reading a bedtime story and getting a big hug and 'I love you, Daddy' just makes the day worthwhile"
>
> - from a father who completed the Father Involvement Survey, child's age 0-4 years

page 55

Father-child involvement

Figure 9.3 **Resources for fathers' questions and concerns about parenting**, based on percentage of responses

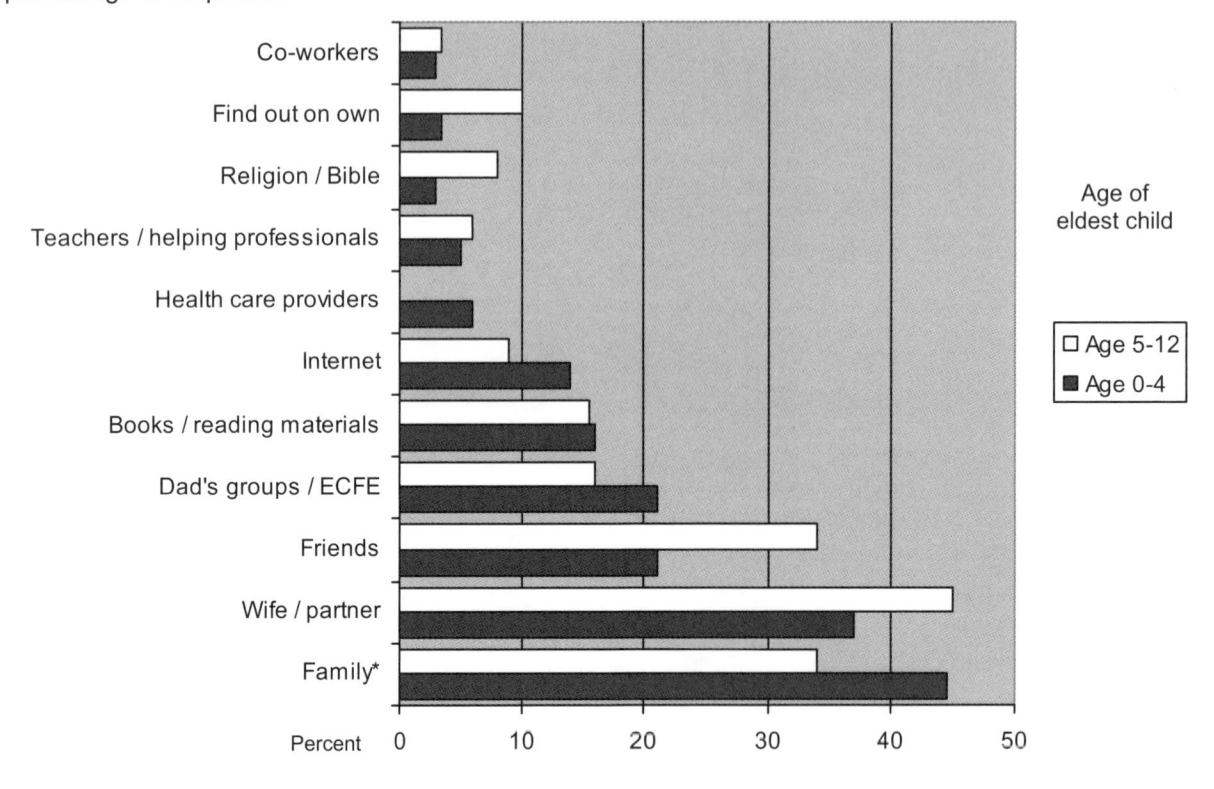

Resource	Age 5-12	Age 0-4
Co-workers	~3	~3
Find out on own	~10	~3
Religion / Bible	~8	~3
Teachers / helping professionals	~6	~5
Health care providers	~0	~6
Internet	~9	~14
Books / reading materials	~15	~16
Dad's groups / ECFE	~16	~21
Friends	~34	~21
Wife / partner	~45	~37
Family*	~34	~45

*Family includes parents, siblings, grandparents, and others.

Part C: Demographic characteristics of the sample population and comparisons to the general population of fathers in Minnesota

Table 9.6 **Ages of fathers who responded to survey**

	Survey respondents: Children's ages 0-4	Survey respondents: Children's ages 5-12
Oldest father	58	62
Youngest father	21	23
Average age of fathers	34.4	37.8

Father-child involvement

Table 9.7 **Race / ethnicity of fathers in survey versus Minnesota**

	Survey respondents: Children's ages 0-4	Survey respondents: Children's ages 5-12	Birth fathers, Minnesota, 2004[1]	Minnesota, total population, 2005[2]
White (Non Hispanic)	83.7%	79.9%	75.6%	86.7%
African American/Black	5.6%	9.4%	6.7%	4.1%
Hispanic	3.0%	3.1%	6.8%	3.5%
Asian	2.3%	2.0%	5.2%	3.4%
Native American	2.0%	2.4%	1.2%	1.2%
Other	3.3%	3.1%	5.8%	N/A

[1] Based on the Minnesota Birth Record information for children born in 2004
[2] Based on 2005 census data for Minnesota

Table 9.7 suggests that the MFFN survey represents a diverse group of fathers with a mixture of White fathers that is similar (79.90% - 83.7%) to the numbers from other sources about race/ethnicity in the state. The percent of certain minority groups (Black & Native American) suggests that there is a higher percentage of these groups represented in the survey sample and a lower number of Asian and Hispanic fathers as compared to current percentages for these latter two groups reflected in the 2004 Minnesota Birth Records and the 2005 census report data for Minnesota.

Table 9.8 **Education levels of fathers in survey versus Minnesota**

Education levels	Survey respondents: Children's ages 0-4	Survey respondents: Children's ages 5-12	Minnesota fathers, 2004[1]
Did not graduate from high school	2.9%	3.9%	8%
High school graduate or equivalent	10.7%	10.5%	28%
Some college	28.6%	26.8%	25%
4 year college degree/graduate degree	57.8%	58.8%	40%

[1] Birth records from Minnesota, father education levels 2004

Table 9.8 summarizes the levels of educational attainment of fathers in the MFFN survey by the two age groups of children. Both groups appear to have a higher level of fathers in the top education level with close to 60% of fathers with at least a 4 year degree versus 40% of fathers who were recorded on Minnesota birth records during 2004. Educational attainment by fathers is one of the factors that has been connected to higher levels of father involvement and is a clear sample bias in the MFFN survey that should be considered when interpreting the results about the level of father involvement in activities with children.

Father-child involvement

Table 9.9 Marital status of fathers in survey versus Minnesota

Marital status	Survey respondents: Children's ages 0-4	Survey respondents: Children's ages 5-12	Census data Minnesota 2005[1]
Married	83.5%	78.3%	75%[2]
Single/ never married	12.5%	8.7%	
Divorced	2.6%	10.3%	
Widowed	0%	0%	
Other	1.3%	2.8%	

[1] Children under 18 living arrangements in Minnesota, 2005 Census data
[2] The census data does not make a differentiation between different categories of non-married fathers so 25% would fall into the other 4 categories in the table.

The marital status of the fathers is presented in Table 9.9 and suggests that there are some differences between the two groups of fathers in the MFFN survey with more fathers of younger children represented in the single/never married category and more fathers with older children in the divorced category. In comparison with fathers of children under 18 there are more married father families in the MFFN sample that can be partially explained by the lower age levels of the children. As children get older they are more likely to experience a divorce so the census data that includes children up to age 18 would reflect a higher level of single parent families through the higher number of divorces for families with children 13-18 years of age. The number of non-residential fathers in the sample is also lower than might be expected with 6% of oldest children in the 0-4 age group living with fathers 40% of the time or less and 15% of the 5-12 age group living with fathers 40% of the time or less. The fathers who do not have children living with them 50% of the time are more difficult to contact and are probably under-represented by the sample.

Table 9.10 Community type of fathers: Survey respondents versus Minnesota

Community Type	Survey respondents: Children's ages 0-4	Survey respondents: Children's ages 5-12	Minnesota, overall population[1]
Urban (big city)	24.4%	27.5%	28.6% (urban: in central place)
Suburbs	38.1%	32.5%	26.5% (urban: not in central place)
Small town 5,000- 60,000	21.5%	22.7%	19% (urban cluster: 2,500—50,000)
Small town / rural	16.0%	17.3%	25.8% (rural: less than 2,500)

[1] U.S. Census Bureau, Census 2000 Summary File 1: GCT-P1.

In Table 9.10 the community environments for fathers who participated in the survey are listed in four different geographic categories. The distribution across the four categories suggests a fairly equal distribution across each type. This indicates that the MFFN network was successful at recruiting fathers across the state in different sizes and types of communities with an over-representation of suburban fathers and an under-representation of fathers from rural areas.

Father-child involvement

The number and ages of children who were reported by fathers of 0-4 year olds and 5-12 year olds are summarized in Figures 9.4 and 9.5. The total number of children represented by the survey sample was 949. The majority of fathers in the survey had young families with 1-2 children.

Figure 9.4 **Children represented in the survey: Ages of eldest children 0-4**

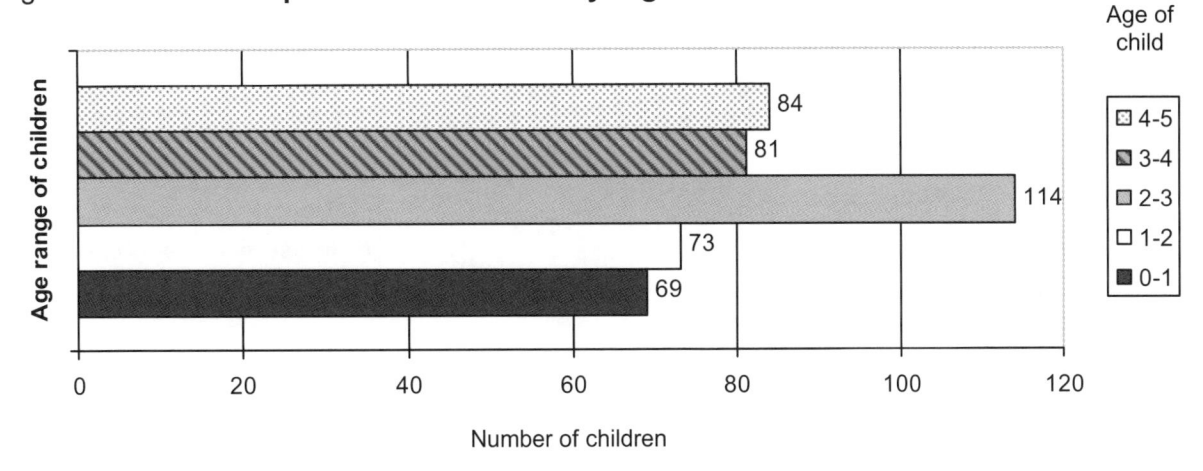

Age of child	Number of children
4-5	84
3-4	81
2-3	114
1-2	73
0-1	69

Figure 9.5 **Children represented in the survey: Ages of eldest children 5-12**

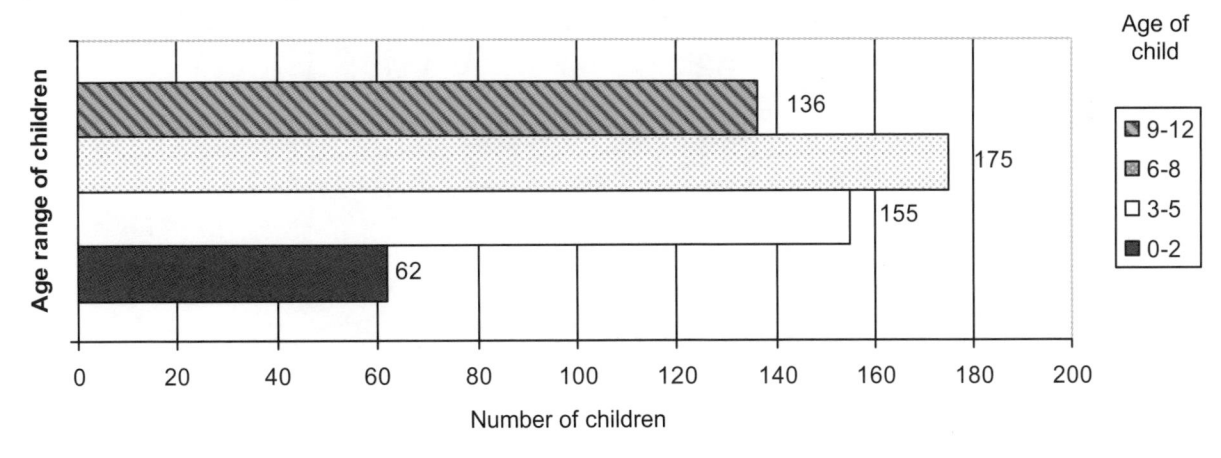

Age of child	Number of children
9-12	136
6-8	175
3-5	155
0-2	62

The MFFN survey of father involvement appears to represent a culturally diverse sample from across the state of Minnesota. The family structures represented also are similar to current state-wide demographics for family structures with children under 18. The major sample bias is in the area of educational attainment of the fathers. The fathers in the survey sample have a significantly higher proportion of highly educated men (60% have four-year or higher degrees). In addition, the sample also over represents fathers who have chosen to participate in parenting/ fatherhood education and support programs and fathers from suburban communities. These sample characteristics will influence the level and types of involvement that are represented in the survey results.

Father-child involvement

Part D: Comparisons with state and national data sources

The following measures reflect additional factors that influence father-child involvement. These figures are from independent sources, as cited.

Figure 9.6 Activities with children younger than 5 years old: Based on fathers' education
Percentage of fathers 15-44 years old who did the specified activity every day in the last 4 weeks with their children, under 5 years old, by father's educational attainment; U.S., 2002

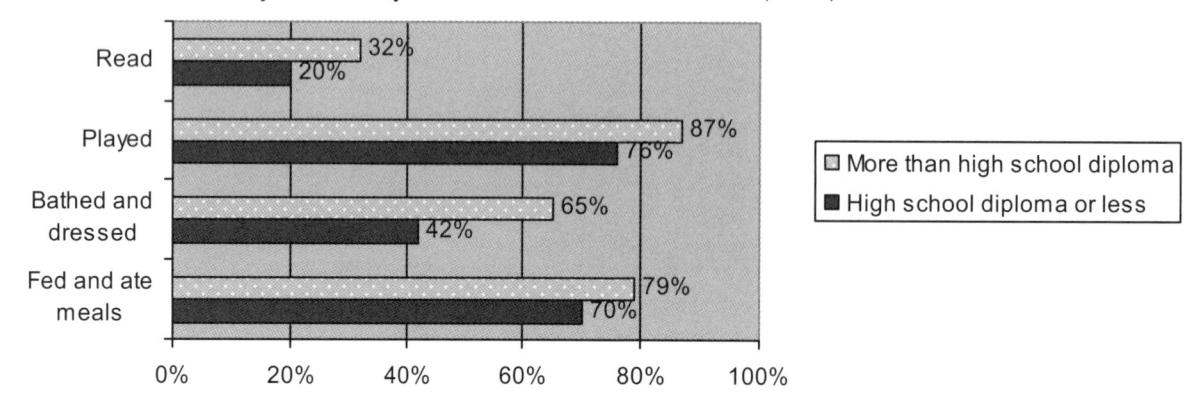

Activity	More than high school diploma	High school diploma or less
Read	32%	20%
Played	87%	76%
Bathed and dressed	65%	42%
Fed and ate meals	79%	70%

Figure 9.7 Activities with children younger than 5 years old: Based on fathers' residence
Percentage of fathers 15-44 years old who did the specified activity every day in the last 4 weeks with their children, under 5 years old, by whether or not they lived with their children; U.S., 2002

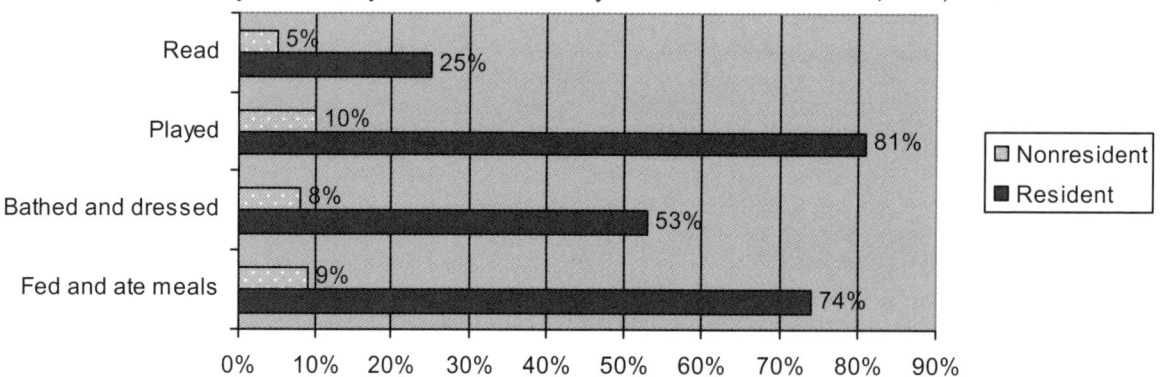

Activity	Nonresident	Resident
Read	5%	25%
Played	10%	81%
Bathed and dressed	8%	53%
Fed and ate meals	9%	74%

SOURCE: Martinex G.M., Chandra A., Abma J. C., Jones J., Mosher W. D. (2006). Fertility, Contraception, and Fatherhood: Data on Men and Women. *From cycle 6 (2002) of the National Survey of Family Growth,* 23(26).

Fathers' education and residential status play an important mediating role in their level of involvement in typical caretaking and parent-child interactions. "Research has shown that fathers, no matter what their income or cultural background, can play a critical role in their children's education. When fathers are involved, their children learn more, perform better in school, and exhibit healthier behavior. Even when fathers do not share a home with their children, their active involvement can have a lasting and positive impact."

SOURCE: U.S. Department of Education & U.S. Department of Health and Human Services. (2000). *A call to commitment: fathers' involvement in children's learning* (DOE Publication No. ED-99-PO-35580). Jessup, MD: Editorial Publications Center.

Father-child involvement

Figure 9.8 **How dads define fatherhood**: Qualities that fathers think are most important for their child (under age 13) to learn

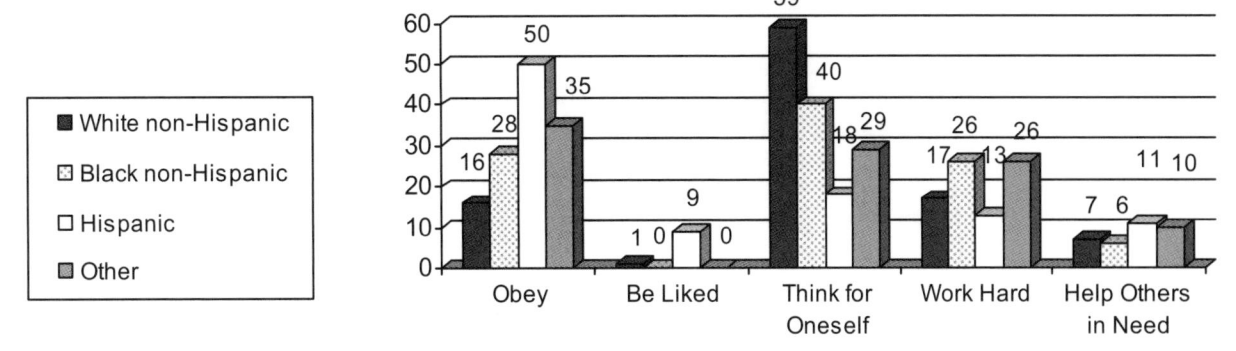

- White non-Hispanic
- Black non-Hispanic
- Hispanic
- Other

Quality	White non-Hispanic	Black non-Hispanic	Hispanic	Other
Obey	16	28	50	35
Be Liked	1	0	9	0
Think for Oneself	59	40	18	29
Work Hard	17	26	13	26
Help Others in Need	7	6	11	10

SOURCE: Panel Study of Income Dynamics. (n.d.). *Child Development Supplement, 1997 [Data File]*. Available from Panel Study of Income Dynamics Data: http://www.psidonline.esr.umich.edu/CDS/

Cultural values are also important and influence fathers' level and type of involvement as reflected in Fig. 9.8.

Figure 9.9 **Parental communication: Father vs. mother**, Minnesota, 2004
Minnesota's students were asked, "Can you talk to your father / mother about problems you are having?" Responses indicate combined percentage of students answering "yes, most of the time" and "yes, some of the time," by gender of student and grade in school.

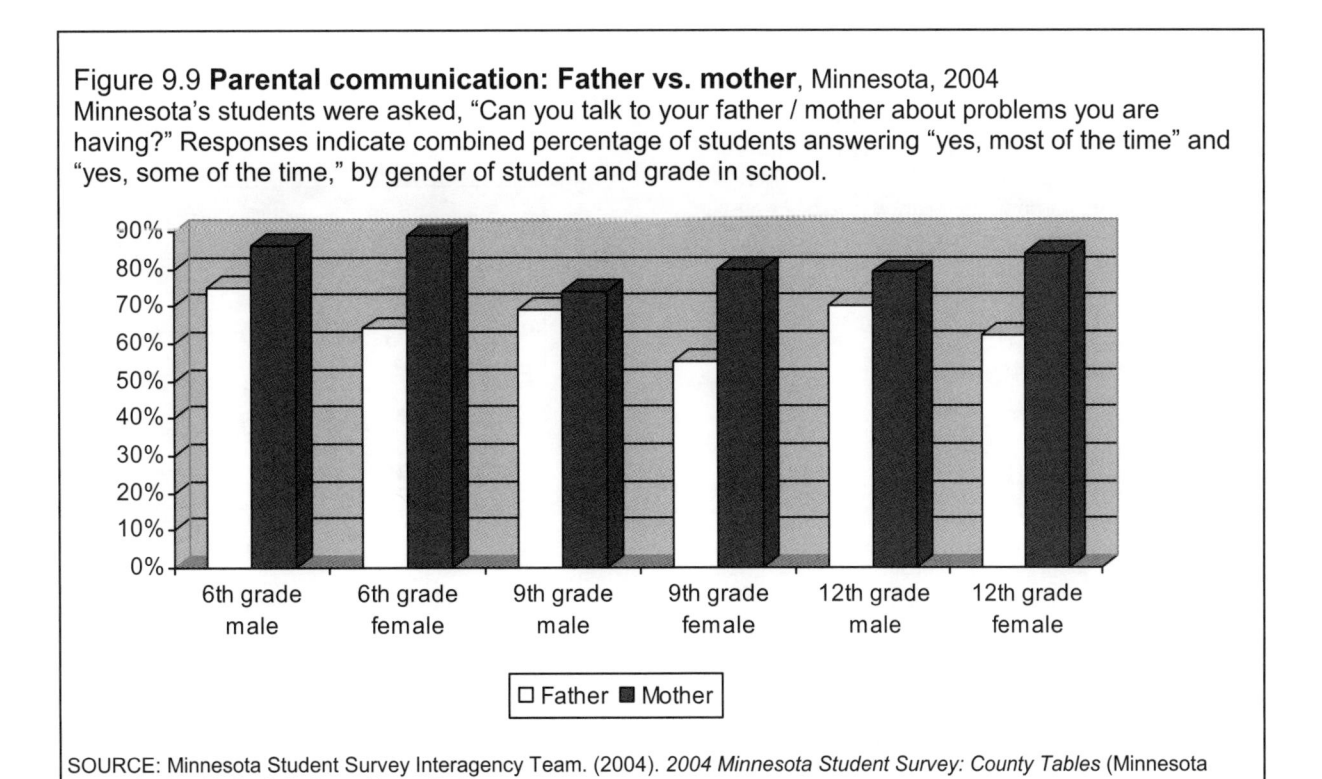

☐ Father ■ Mother

SOURCE: Minnesota Student Survey Interagency Team. (2004). *2004 Minnesota Student Survey: County Tables* (Minnesota Center for Health Statistics). annkinney@state.mn.us.
Approximately 66% of all Minnesota students participated in the survey in grades 6, 9 and 12 in public operating school districts.

According to Minnesota's students, more boys and girls can talk with their mothers than with their fathers. It is interesting to note that 9th grade boys and girls have a harder time than 6th graders or 12th graders talking to their fathers.

Father-child involvement

Unmarried fathers: Lower levels of father-child involvement

"After the declaration of paternity, the bedrock of fathering is presence in the child's life. The two major structural threats to fathers' presence are nonmarital childbearing and divorce.

"In nearly all cases, children born outside of marriage reside with their mothers. If fathers do not live with the mother and child, their presence in the child's life is frequently marginal, and even when active for a time, tends to be fragile over time.

"The quality of the father-child relations both inside and outside marriage is more strongly correlated with the quality of the coparental relationship than is true for the mother-child relationship.

"One reason that fathering is particularly sensitive to the marital or coparental relationship is that standards and expectations for fathering appear to be more variable than those for mothering. There is more negotiation in families of what fathers will do than what mothers will do, and hence more dependence among fathers on the quality and outcome of those negotiations."

SOURCE: Doherty, W. J., Kouneski, E. F., & Erickson, M. F. (1996). *Responsible Fathering: An overview and conceptual framework.* (HHS-100-93-0012). Washington DC: Administration for Children and Families.

Religion and fatherhood

One set of measures of father-child involvement revolves around religion and moral guidance. According to W. Bradford Wilcox, "Parents who participate in church activities are more likely to value obedience in their children than other parents [and] are more likely to be involved with their children's education". Furthermore, Wilcox states, "Fathers who attend church frequently are more likely to monitor their children, to praise and hug their children, and to spend time with their children. Thus, religious participation, which is understood here as an indicator of religiosity, would seem to foster an authoritative, active, and expressive style of parenting" (Wilcox, 2002).

According to a ChildTrends research brief, "Evidence suggests that mothers' personal religious practices are a more powerful predictor of children's religiosity than are those of their fathers. Yet, at the same time, research suggests that a significant portion of men express a deeper commitment to religion and a greater involvement in religious activities after becoming fathers." The research brief goes on to say, "As with many other kinds of parental involvement, data show that fathers who are college graduates are more likely to engage their children in religious activities than fathers who have gone less far in school" (ChildTrends, 2001).

The Best Part of Being a Dad

"Seeing my children excel at something or seeing their interest or quest for knowledge and helping them with that. Constantly being challenged and always being loved."

- from a father who completed the Father Involvement Survey, child's age 5-12 years

Father-child involvement

Part E: Methodology of Father Involvement Survey

A review of the existing research revealed a number of national studies over the last 10 years but very limited information on fathers in Minnesota. A decision was made to conduct a survey of fathers in Minnesota to assess the current level of father involvement. A statewide telephone survey of fathers as a vehicle to gather this information would have been cost prohibitive. Instead of a phone survey, the authors chose a second option, which was to conduct a survey via Internet and using the MFFN network and to reach fathers around the state with paper copies of the survey instrument. This chapter presented the preliminary results of the survey and uses data from recent national studies as a comparative framework for understanding father involvement in Minnesota.

The purpose of the survey was to find out more about how men of young children (ages 0-4) and school aged children (ages 5-12) think about fathering and how they perceive their level of involvement in typical parenting tasks for these two age groups. Past surveys often have failed to consider changing child needs in their exploration of father involvement by including all children under age 18 and using a generic set of parenting activities.

The methodology used was a non-probability convenience sample with some snowball characteristics. The MFFN network served as a primary contact with fatherhood programs around the state. The authors also used other related organizations such as the Minnesota Council on Family Relations (MCFR) and the Minnesota Association of Family and Early Educators (MNAFEE) to publicize the survey.

The survey was available as an Internet survey that could be answered online and as a paper survey that could be passed out to individuals or to classes and then returned to MFFN. The survey was conducted for about 6 weeks from the beginning of October through mid-November, 2006. There were a total of 567 surveys that were completed during this time. There were 310 completed by fathers of 0-4 year old children and 257 completed by fathers of 5-12 year olds. The results suggest that the survey represents a wide range of fathers from across the state of Minnesota. The major bias factor may be that many of the fathers were recruited through fatherhood and parenting education programs and represent fathers who have a higher level of education and are more involved in their children's lives than the typical Minnesota father.

Chapter 10 Services and programs for Minnesota's fathers

Figure 10.1 **Minnesota's regional fatherhood service providers**, number of responses to spring 2006 program survey, by region of state

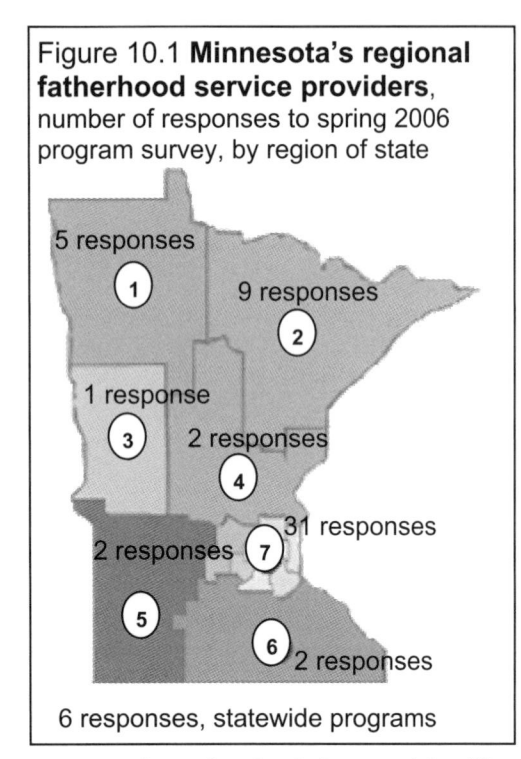

- Region 1: 5 responses
- Region 2: 9 responses
- Region 3: 1 response
- Region 4: 2 responses
- Region 5: 2 responses
- Region 6: 2 responses
- Region 7: 31 responses
- 6 responses, statewide programs

The Minnesota Fathers & Families Network (MFFN), in conjunction with State Cloud State University, conducted a survey of father related services by contacting providers throughout the State of Minnesota. Minnesota is divided into seven regional districts with a varying number of father related service providers in each region. Seven of the providers posted on the MFFN website are listed as providing statewide services over all seven regions. While others offer services in the region they are located.

The purpose of the survey was to identify the types of services provided and the availability of services to fathers in Minnesota. The survey started out by asking if the organization contacted did provide services aimed at meeting the needs of fathers in their community. Of the 58 responses, all the providers stated that they did provide services to fathers.

The survey focused on eight services deemed important to fathers. The list of services was developed at a brainstorming meeting in January of 2006 by the members of an Oversight Committee which consisted of educators, government agency representatives, and members of private groups advocating for fathers and families (see listing of Oversight Committee members at the end of this document). The meeting designated eight service areas related to fathers they saw as pertinent factors in meeting the needs of fathers in Minnesota to be included in the survey: **family law, parent education, healthcare/health education, employment, mental health, supervised parenting time (visitation), father-child related activities, and support groups**. The 58 respondents to the survey were asked if they offered any of the eight services by replying yes or no. The following chart illustrates the eight services and the number of providers throughout Minnesota offering services to fathers from the 58 respondents participating in the survey (respondents are listed at the end of this document).

Figure 10.2 **Number of agencies providing each type of service to Minnesota's fathers,** from the responses of 58 social service / educational programs surveyed, spring 2006

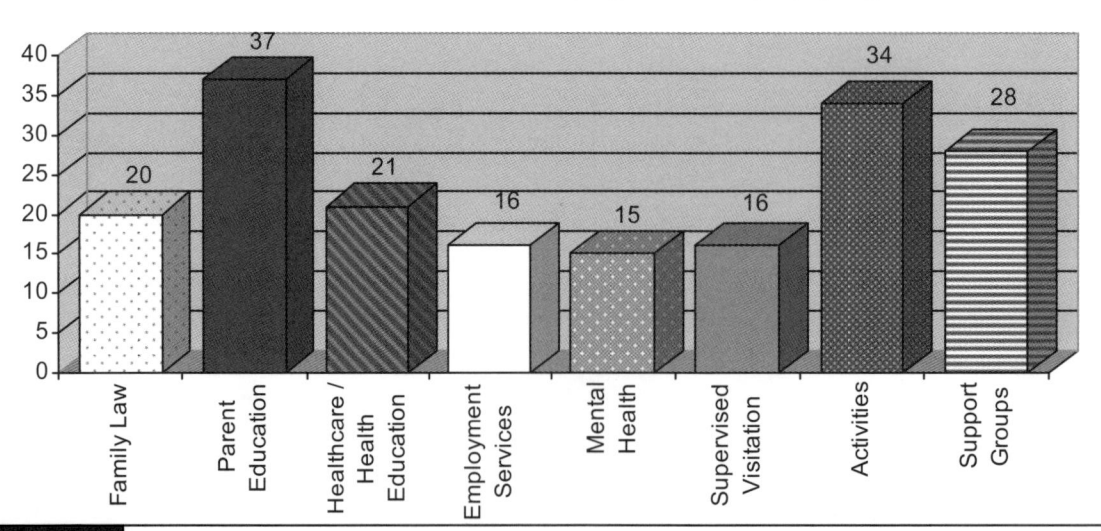

Service	Number
Family Law	20
Parent Education	37
Healthcare / Health Education	21
Employment Services	16
Mental Health	15
Supervised Visitation	16
Activities	34
Support Groups	28

page 64

Services and programs for Minnesota's fathers

Along with the types of services the providers offered, they were also asked the number of fathers they served and the gender of the persons providing the service. Almost none of the 58 respondents kept track of the exact number of fathers they served in the past year. Forty-one providers of father related services gave estimations of the number of fathers they served during the past year. Seventeen refrained from giving estimated numbers of fathers served. The estimated total from the number of fathers served by the 41 respondents to this question was 16,687 with the low of 9 fathers served to the high of 6,100 fathers served, per organization. The average of fathers served was approximately 417 per organization with a median and mode of 100. The following graph illustrates the number of fathers served per organization. Four agencies served more than 1,000 fathers.

The gender of the personnel providing the services among the 58 respondents was 75 males and 180 females. The numbers for gender and number of persons providing services to fathers are rough estimates as provided by the 58 respondents.

Methodology

A telephone survey of service providers to fathers was conducted during the months of March and April. The list of 105 service providers was obtained from the Minnesota Fathers and Families website and the service providers were contacted by telephone throughout the two month period. All of the providers except four were contacted by phone. The four who were unavailable were called at the number listed on the Minnesota Fathers and Family website, but a recording was reached in each instance stating the number was disconnected or no longer in service. A Google search was conducted of the names and/or the addresses of the four providers which proved inconclusive as to the current status of the four providers or their whereabouts.

Figure 10.4 **Gender of staff serving fathers**

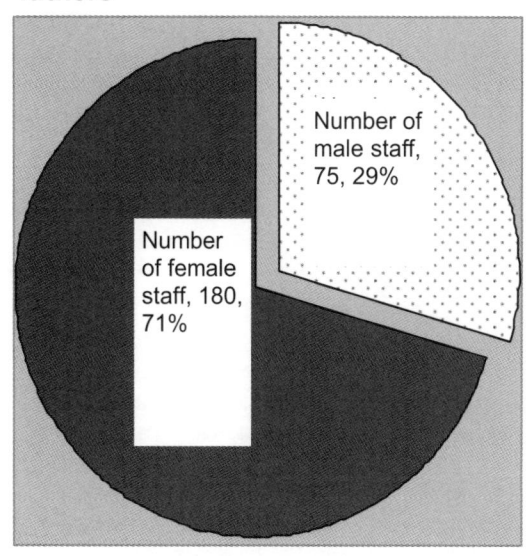

- Number of male staff, 75, 29%
- Number of female staff, 180, 71%

Figure 10.3 **Size of fatherhood programs**
Responses to the question, "How many fathers do you serve annually?"

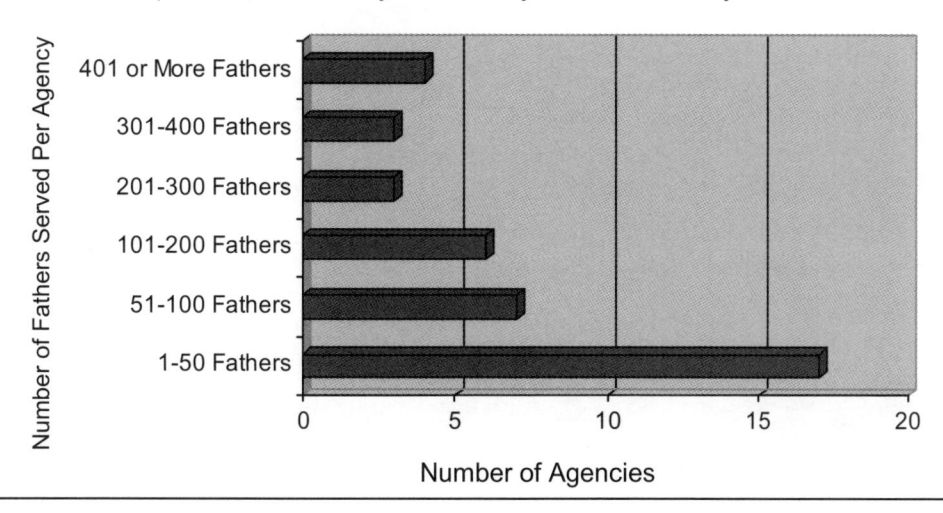

Number of Fathers Served Per Agency	Number of Agencies
401 or More Fathers	4
301-400 Fathers	3
201-300 Fathers	3
101-200 Fathers	6
51-100 Fathers	7
1-50 Fathers	17

Services and programs for Minnesota's fathers

The remaining service providers were called three times unless they had responded when previously called. Upon the third phone call, a message was left explaining the survey and a phone number where they could participate in the survey should they decide to contact us. Of the 101 services providers contacted, 58 replied, 2 declined participation, and 41 did not reply.

Discussion

Although the survey focused on eight specific services affecting fathers in Minnesota, the boundaries between them and other services are ill-defined according to discussions which took place while interviewing the 58 survey respondents. Many stated that, although they might not offer one of the services listed on the survey, they may address some aspect of the eight services on a limited basis based on the need of the individual father and/or capability the provider had to assist the father. Referral to another agency better equipped to provide the services needed was also noted by the majority of the respondents when working with fathers.

An issue which surfaced regularly through discourse with the respondents revolved around the anger of the fathers with whom they worked. Dialogue regarding mental health issues and support groups precipitated concerns over a lack of resources devoted to the teaching and maintenance of anger management skills for fathers. They expressed doubt that fathers in the system could change their current circumstances unless some types of anger management services are made available.

Figure 10.5 **Number of survey responses**

Respondents included staff or volunteers associated with programs listed on the "Minnesota Fathers' Services Directory".

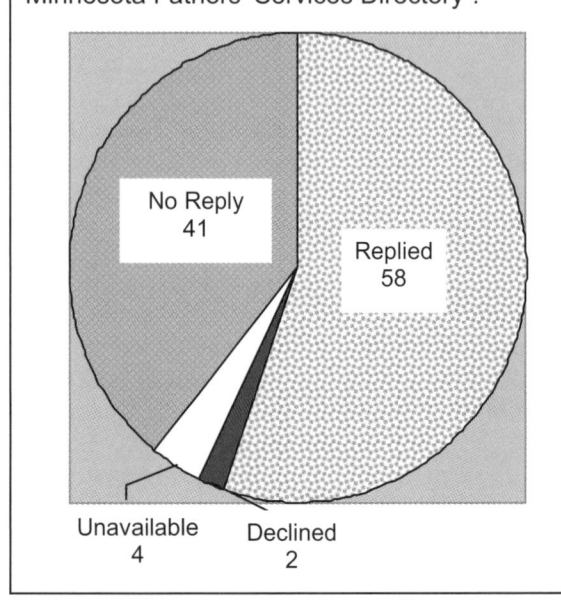

- No Reply 41
- Replied 58
- Unavailable 4
- Declined 2

The respondents echoed sentiments that the tracking of fathers, particularly their numbers in relation to services fathers receive, needs to be improved because the data is grossly underreported and fails to portray an accurate account of what services are provided fathers in Minnesota. A common theme among the respondents was the need for the implementation of a statewide data bank collecting and processing information about fathers and the types of services available to them in Minnesota. The Minnesota Fathers & Families Network has maintained an online database, the "Fathers' Services Directory", for the past three years; clearly respondents would like to see this database expanded, both in the types of services described and in the accessibility of this resource to fathers and fatherhood professionals across the state.

The Best Part of Being a Dad

"The fact that I have a daughter. The fact that I have a family. These facts mentally support me as a man and a human and make me stronger in life. [She] motivates me to be more responsible and to strive to be my best."

- from a father who completed the Father Involvement Survey, child's age 0-4 years

section three

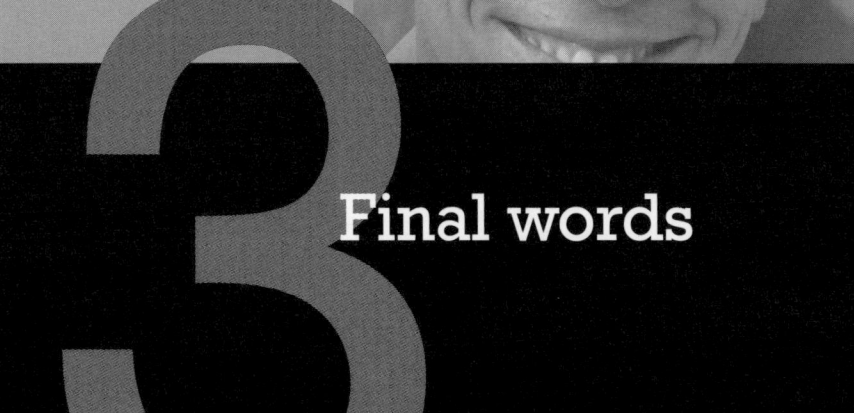

3 Final words

Initial Recommendations — Chapter 11

In this chapter, the authors begin to draw initial conclusions from the report and to make basic recommendations. These recommendations are divided into three categories: data and research, fatherhood services, and public policy and education.

These recommendations are meant to initiate further thoughtful analysis by every reader. These recommendations are, in no manner, an exhaustive list of "next steps".

Throughout 2007 and beyond, the Minnesota Fathers & Families Network will utilize this report to build on our knowledge of fatherhood within our organizational work, in social services programs, and in the public and private sectors. We hope that you will join us in our effort to broaden, to edit, and to implement these recommendations — in an effort to increase our understanding of fatherhood in Minnesota and to improve the well-being of Minnesota's fathers, families, and children.

I. Data and research: Let's count Minnesota's fathers.

The following recommendations point to the need for more comprehensive collection of data as it relates to fathers in Minnesota. In many cases the authors were able to get frustratingly-close to locating information about fathers — but had to settle with data about men or information about parents. At the same time, the available data was in some situations quite complex — but only examined a very narrow population of fathers or a limited sample. Additionally, the authors learned that many fathers are invisible to data collection at different points in the lives of children, either by the choice of the father or another family member or by the lack of surveys that could reveal this information.

On the other hand, recent research and data collection have not been entirely devoid of information about fathers. Statistics gathered in this publication reveal important trends in Minnesota related to father well-being including valuable information about changing family structures and a rise in single fatherhood, a link between fathers' education and child-bearing, a broader understanding of multiple-partner fertility and its impact on the economic status of families, and a better understanding that minority fathers are undercounted at various points in the lives of children.

Primary recommendation: Conduct a longitudinal study of a cohort of fathers and children: Minnesota would be well-served by a long-term study of a representative group of fathers and children, from birth through adolescence/adulthood. This study could provide a fascinating and valuable picture of the different impacts on child development based on paternity establishment, child-father attachment, living circumstances, and more. A longitudinal study of fathers and children in Minnesota would be a historic piece of research with implications for public policy, research, and social service programming.

Count parents, not just "adults": State government agencies and state-funded projects would be more responsive to community interests and needs if they would track parents, when possible, during enrollment to government-sponsored programs and services. For example, the University of Minnesota Extension Services' 4-H youth program already reports statistics about adult male and female volunteers, but not mothers and fathers. Similarly, the Minnesota Department of Corrections has extensive information about inmates, but lacks a clear picture of the number of incarcerated fathers.

Count moms and dads, not just "parents": State agencies would gain a clearer picture of the

> We hope that you will join the Minnesota Fathers & Families Network in our effort to broaden, to edit, and to implement these recommendations — in an effort to increase our understanding of fatherhood in Minnesota and to improve the well-being of Minnesota's fathers, families, and children.

Initial Recommendations

involvement and roles of both parents if they would track and disseminate information about mothers and fathers individually. Currently, various data points are recorded solely as "parent" without statistics about gender.

Count young fathers independently, not just "teen mothers": Young fathers are often identified as "fathers of children born to teen mothers." The failure to directly and independently count and serve teen fathers discounts the roles that young men play in their own economic and educational success and in that of their families and children.

Simplify definitions of fatherhood: While motherhood is fairly static in its definition, fatherhood is an evolving and ambiguous concept. The variety of definitions —including legal father, biological father, putative father, and many others — creates a landscape of uncertainty for men, especially for unmarried or divorced fathers. All family members would benefit from simplified definitions of fatherhood.

Seek one definition of "single father": Currently, single fatherhood includes men who live alone with their children as well as men who may live with an unmarried adult partner. The lack of a uniform definition complicates the development of effective programs to meet the needs of these families.

II. Fatherhood Services: Let's support healthy father-child relationships.

The recommendations in this section point to the need for more intervention and prevention services for fathers — especially for men who are young, unmarried, or low-income. The many challenges fathers describe in the survey, Chapter 9, suggest that a change in culture in this area might help to prepare fathers for these challenges with greater attention to both parent education and support. It is assumed that fathers will instinctively know or muddle through the transition to fatherhood with little or no support. These recommendations seek to make it easier for men to connect with their children and to stay connected to their children in healthy and meaningful ways.

Primary recommendation: Develop a mechanism for state-funding of programs that promote healthy fatherhood: Minnesota is fortunate to have over 100 programs that offer a variety of services for the state's fathers. These programs, as well as programs for women and children, should be able to count on a portion of their funding from a reliable revenue stream. Communities with higher levels of "fathers in the shadows", as well as underserved small towns and rural communities, would benefit from state funding for healthy fatherhood programming.

Primary recommendation: Address social burdens of multiple-partner fertility and unmarried births: Minnesota would benefit from broad solutions that combine both early intervention and prevention policies on a cross-sectoral basis including education/job skills training, sexuality education, family planning, violence prevention, healthy relationship skills development and marriage promotion. Additional recommendations related to this topic are listed individually, below.

Support education and job skills training for men in fragile families: Young fathers, low-income fathers and fathers who have lower levels of education would benefit from easier access to employment training programs, educational advancement, and culturally competent social/professional support networks. These services would increase the capacity of fathers to financially provide for their children and to serve as positive role models.

> **The Best Part of Being a Dad**
>
> "watching my daughter grow and develop into a fine young lady who has morals, values and respect for others"
>
> - from a father who completed the Father Involvement Survey, child's age 5-12 years

Initial Recommendations

Support incarcerated fathers to maintain healthy families: The rates of incarceration among children of incarcerated parents are disproportionately higher than among the general population. This fact demonstrates the need to help incarcerated men to develop and maintain healthy relationships with their children, when appropriate, during their incarceration and upon re-entry into the community. More programs are needed to help fathers break the generational cycle of incarceration.

Strengthen the state's early childhood programs for families: Early Childhood Family Education (ECFE) and Early Head Start are educational programs offered to families across Minnesota. Recognizing that parents are a child's first and most significant teachers, these programs offer a variety of classes and resources for parents and children birth through kindergarten age. These classes are often the only source of formal support that many parents receive for learning how to raise their children and to prepare them for success in school. Minnesota would be well-served if higher percentages of fathers were to take advantage of these valuable resources in all corners of the state.

III. Public Policy and Education: Let's embrace the ideal of healthy fatherhood.

All segments of the population must embrace the promotion of healthy fatherhood. The media, public policy makers, and the general public can each play a significant role defining healthy fatherhood. Collaboratively, we can help Minnesota's children to experience a loving connection to fathers of all types – biological, foster, adoptive, social, psychological – and start seeing men as a vital component of healthy childhood, healthy family life, and healthy communities.

Primary recommendation: Develop a state-level office/position to track the well-being of fatherhood: The State of Minnesota would benefit from the creation of a state-level office which would ensure that government agencies are tracking the health and well-being of all family members. Across the nation, a majority of all states have staffed a state-supported government agency, office, or task force that is charged with promoting greater support for positive father involvement through state agencies and policies.

Primary recommendation: Embrace a healthy view of male socialization: Male socialization, the concept of how boys learn what it means to be male, is a complex societal process. Minnesotans would benefit from the promotion of more healthy messages of manhood that prepare boys for fatherhood and family life. This would require a cultural shift to focus on the ethic of healthy/responsible fatherhood and to focus on the prevention of absent or uninvolved fatherhood. This cultural shift would require a change in media/cultural portrayals of acceptable male behaviors, less aggression, less degradation of women, more expression of emotion, and more examples of nurturing fathers.

Encourage more men to work in social services and educational settings: Among the programs surveyed in Chapter 10, women comprise more than two-thirds of all staff that work with fathers. Educational and social service programs in Minnesota would be well-served by recruiting and hiring more men in direct-service roles. This change would help boys, girls, men and women to value this work and to view social services and education as gender-neutral professions.

Encourage boys to participate in early childhood development education and activities: Boys would grow in their capacity to be nurturant men and healthy fathers if schools and youth groups, such as the Boy Scouts or 4-H, were to encourage boys of all ages to participate in family life education classes and infant/child development activities. In addition to supporting the individual boys' personal development, these opportunities may lead more young men to pursue college and careers in the social service and educational fields.

Support education for adolescents and young adults to prevent too early parenthood: Minnesota's youth benefit in many ways from parent education programs and educational opportunities that help them to understand the importance of being ready to become a parent, the challenges of parenting at a

Initial Recommendations

young age, and the options they have for avoiding risky behaviors. The Dads Make a Difference program is one strong example of a proven curriculum being carried out in various Minnesota school districts.

Promote health and mental health for men: Issues related to health and mental health have been traditionally down-played among men and within fathers' groups. The rates of male suicide, depression, and domestic violence must be addressed more openly. Minnesota cannot promote the well-being of fatherhood without embracing the well-being of men. Men and families would achieve improved well-being if Minnesota's men were to embrace more open dialogue about health and mental health issues.

Engage in dialogue about violence prevention: Within the field of fatherhood work, anger management classes are an important resource for men. Often, these classes are the only option available to meet a variety of individual needs among men coming from distinct situations. Men's programs could share strategies and learn lessons through the development of stronger collaborations with programs that address child abuse, dating violence, domestic abuse, and sexual violence.

Promote marriage as an important resource for strengthening families: Research shows that children who are raised in low-conflict married two-parent households achieve well in academic and social settings. Marriage is an important resource for early childhood development. At the same time, family stability, in all family structures, is an important goal that has been under-emphasized.

Support families who are not married and may face additional barriers to positive parenting: Many of the strengths accrued to children through marriage may not be due to the marriage itself, but rather to the host of benefits that society endows to married couples. Families that choose not to marry or who are not allowed to marry may face social barriers that are not, by definition or necessity, entwined with the act of marriage.

Recognize the reality that many fathers have children in more than one household: Men who have experienced multiple-partner fertility (fathers with children living in more than one household) are difficult to track, difficult to count, and often absent in discussions about healthy fatherhood. As the field of fatherhood continues to mature, it will be increasingly important to recognize the unique situations of these fathers, the challenges of fulfilling the role of father among various homes — especially the financial demands to provide for two or more households — and the difficulty of co-parenting with the mothers of their children.

Educate men about all options for paternity establishment and for protecting their rights as fathers: Unmarried fathers have a variety of options to establish paternity and to gain healthy access to their children. The state currently provides a financial incentive to hospitals when fathers sign a Recognition of Parentage upon the birth of the child. The state would be well-served by broadening this incentive to include all options for men to establish paternity or to protect their rights as putative fathers including the Recognition of Parentage, Fathers' Adoption Registry, and genetic testing.

Expand access to information about the Fathers' Adoption Registry: The FAR, a valuable tool for unmarried putative fathers to keep informed about their children, is underutilized by Minnesota's fathers. Increased state funding would be well-utilized to educate men about the FAR as a limited option for protecting their rights as putative fathers.

Bibliography and Acknowledgements — Chapter 12

Bibliography

American Journal of Public Health. (2006). Marriage boosts parents' mental health [Electronic version]. *Forbes Magazine*. Online, September 28, 2006.

Annie E. Casey Foundation. (2005). *State profiles of child well-being: 2005 kids count data book*. Baltimore, MD: Annie E. Casey Foundation.

Avenilla, F., Rosenthal, E., and Tice, P. (2006). *Fathers of U.S. children born in 2001: Findings from the early childhood longitudinal study, birth cohort* (NCES 2006-002). U.S. Department of Education, National Center for Education Statistics. Washington, DC: U.S. Government Printing Office.

Blankenhorn, D. (1995). *Fatherless America: Confronting our most urgent social problem*. New York: Basic Books.

Chase, R., Arnold, J., Schauben, L., and Shardlow, B. (February 2006). *Family Friend and Neighbor Caregivers: Results of the 2004 Minnesota statewide household child care survey*. St. Paul: Wilder Research.

Children's Defense Fund Minnesota. (2000). *Minnesota Children and the 2000 Census: Housing and Family*. Retrieved March 12, 2006 from http://www.cdf-mn.org/CensusData2000/MNChildHousing.pdf

Child Welfare League of America. (2006). *Minnesota's Children 2006*. Retrieved July 20, 2006 from http://www.cwla.org/advoacy/statefactsheets/2006minnesota.htm

Conner, M. E., & White, J. L. (2006). *Black fathers: An invisible presence in America*. Mahwah, NJ: Lawrence Eribaum Associates.

Doherty, W. J., Kouneski, E. F., & Erickson, M. F. (1996). *Responsible Fathering: An overview and conceptual framework*. (HHS-100-93-0012). Washington DC: Administration for Children and Families.

Gillaspy, T. (personal communication, September 19, 2006). Minnesota's active military fathers. Message sent to lorenn@albanytel.com, archived at lorenn@albanytel.com

Giveans, D., & Robinson, M. (1992). Old and new images of fatherhood. In C. S. Scull (Ed.), *Fathers, sons, and daughters: Exploring fatherhood, renewing the bond*. Los Angeles: Jeremy P. Tarcher.

Grall, T (2003). *Custodial Mothers and Fathers and Their Child Support: 2001*. Retrieved December 15, 2006 from Child Trends DataBank: http://www.childtrendsdatabank.org/indicators/84ChildSupport.cfm

Halle, T. (2002). *Charting parenthood: A statistical portrait of fathers and mothers in America*. Retrieved January 2, 2007, from http://www.childtrends.org/Files/ParenthoodRpt2002.pdf

---

The Most Challenging Part of Being a Dad

Finding the balance between giving my son everything he needs versus spoiling him.

- from a father who completed the Father Involvement Survey, child's age 0-4 years

Bibliography and Acknowledgements

Hennepin County Office of Planning and Development. (2002). *African American men project: Crossroads, Choosing a new direction.* Retrieved October 15, 2006, from http://www.planning.org/MerriamLib/2003/dec02jan03.htm

Kelly, E (2005). The impact of work-life policies on families. *Consortium Connections.* 14 (1).

Kozaryn, L. D. (2003). DoD studies mission: Family needs. *American Forces Press Service.* Retrieved September 14, 2006, from http://www.defenselink.mil

> **The Best Part of Being a Dad**
>
> "Being able to watch my sons grow up and learn right from wrong as well as responsibility. Instilling values in them that I know will carry them on through life."
>
> - from a father who completed the Father Involvement Survey, child's age 5-12 years

Logan, C., Manlove, J., Ikramullah, E., & Cottingham, S. (2006). *Men who father children with more than one woman: A contemporary portrait of multiple-partner fertility* (Publication No. 2006-10). Washington DC: Child Trends.

Martin, J. A., Brady, H. E., Sutton, P. D., Ventura, S. J., Menacher, F., & Kirmeyer, S. (2006). Births: Final Data for 2004. *National Vital Statistics Report,* 55(1).

Martinex G.M., Chandra A., Abma J. C., Jones J., Mosher W. D. (2006). Fertility, Contraception, and Fatherhood: Data on Men and Women. *From cycle 6 (2002) of the National Survey of Family Growth,* 23(26).

Minnesota Center for Health Statistics. Hajicek, C. (Personal communication, July 21, 2006). *Health Statistics.* Message sent to lorenn@albanytel.com, archived at lorenn@albanytel.com

Minn. Commission on Out-of-School Time. (March 2004). *Demographic Snapshot.* www.mncost.org

Minnesota Department of Administration State Demographic Center (2003). *Minnesota household projections 2000-2030.* Retrieved January 2, 2007, from http://www.demography.state.mn.us

Minnesota Department of Corrections, (2006). Adult inmate profile as of 1/01/2006. Retrieved March 20, 2006, from http://www/doc.state.mn.us

Minnesota Department of Health. (n.d.) *Minnesota Father's Adoption Registry.* Retrieved November 2, 2006 from http://www.health.state.mn.us/divs/chs/registry/top.htm

Minnesota Department of Health. (n.d.) *Minnesota Father's Adoption Registry Questions and Facts.* Retrieved November 2, 2006 from http://www.health.state.mn.us/divs/chs/registry/faq.htm

Minnesota Department of Human Services. Campbell, W. (Personal Communication, December 14, 2006). *Child Support Enforcement Division.* Message sent to info@mnfathers.org, archived at info@mnfathers.org

Minnesota Department of Human Services. Chazdon, S. (Personal Communication, December 15, 2006). *Program Assessment and Integrity Division.* Message sent to info@mnfathers.org, archived at info@mnfathers.org

Bibliography and Acknowledgements

Minnesota Department of Human Services. (2005). *Child support-Establishing parentage.* Retrieved March 16, 2006, from http://www.dhs.state.mn.us/main/groups/children/documents/pub/dhs_id_008808.hcsp

Minnesota Department of Human Services. (n.d.). *Child Support in Minnesota: Facts and figures.* Retrieved January 2, 2006, from http://www.dhs.state.mn.us

Minnesota Department of Human Services. (2005). *Minnesota family investment program longitudinal study: four years after baseline.* St. Paul: Author.

Minnesota Department of Human Services. (2003). *Minnesota family investment program longitudinal study: Special report on teen mothers.* St. Paul: Author.

Minnesota Department of Human Services. (2005). *2005 Minnesota Child and Family Service Reviews* (Quarterly Supervisor's Forum: Engaging and Involving Fathers). Retrieved March 1, 2006, from http://www.dhs.state.mn.us

Minnesota Department of Human Services. (2005). *2005 Minnesota child support: Performance report* (Child Support Enforcement Division). Retrieved March 1, 2006, from http://www.dhs.state.mn.us

Minnesota Department of Human Services. (2005). *Welfare in Minnesota: Facts and figures.* St. Paul: Author.

Minnesota Department of Public Safety, Office of Justice Programs. (2006). *OJP Fact Sheet: Domestic Violence.* St. Paul: Minnesota Department of Public Safety.

Minnesota State Court Administrator's Office. (2005). *Marriage/Divorce Table 1 and 2.* Retrieved November 2, 2006 from http://www.courts.state.mn.us

Minnesota State Demographic Center. (April 2004). *Population Notes: Minnesota's Children in the 2000 Census.* St. Paul: Author.

Minnesota Student Survey Interagency Team. (2004). *2004 Minnesota Student Survey: County Tables* (Minnesota Center for Health Statistics). annkinney@state.mn.us.

National Center for Children in Poverty. (2005). *Family Economic Security: Minnesota State Context.* Retrieved March 20, 2006, from http://www.nccp.org/state_detail_Context_MN.html

National Center for Education Statistics. Statistical data compiled from 2000 Census SF 30003 (P037).

National Center for Injury Prevention and Control, U.S. Centers for Disease Control and Prevention. (September 2006). *Suicide: Fact Sheet.* Retrieved November 12, 2006 from www.cdc.gov/ncipc/factsheets/suifacts.htm

National Fatherhood Initiative. (2004). *Family Structure, Father Closeness, & Drug Abuse.* Gaithersburg MD. Retrieved March 10, 2006, from http://www.fatherhood.org/research.htm

National Survey of Children's Health. (2005). *Child and adolescent health measurement initiative.* Retrieved July 10, 2006 from http://www.nschdata.org/content/ChartbooksPubsAndPresentations.aspx

Office on the Economic Status of Women. (2005). *Minnesota compared to other states and the United States: Summary of the Status of Women Profile Reports.* St. Paul, MN: Author.

Office of the Under Secretary of Defense, (2004). Population representation in the military servives 2004. Retrieved September 15, 2006 from Department of Defense: http://dod.mil

Palkovitz, R. (1997). Reconstructing "involvement": Expanding conceptualizations of men's caring in contemporary families. In A.J.

Bibliography and Acknowledgements

Hawkins & D.C. Dollahite (Eds.), *Generative fathering: Beyond deficit perspectives* (pp. 200-216). Thousand Oaks, CA: Sage.

Panel Study of Income Dynamics. (n.d.). *Child Development Supplement, 1997 [Data File]*. Available from Panel Study of Income Dynamics Data: http://www.psidonline.esr.umich.edu/CDS/

Prevent Child Abuse Minnesota. (n.d.). *Child abuse prevention materials*. Retrieved August 12, 2006, from http://www.pcamn.org

Remington, M. R. (October-December, 2006). Second time around: Grandparents raising children. *Family Times*.

Rosenberg, J. & Wilcox, W.B. (2006). *The importance of fathers in the healthy development of children*. Washington DC: U.S. Office on Child Abuse and Neglect.

Strauss, Murray A., Gelles, Richard J. and Smith, Christine. (1990). Physical Violence in American Families; Risk Factors and Adaptations to Violence in 8,145 Families. New Brunswick: Transaction Publishers in *The facts on domestic violence*. San Francisco: Family Violence Prevention Fund. http://www.endabuse.org

Travis, J. (2005). *But they all come back: Facing the challenges of prisoner reentry*. Washington, DC: The Urban Institute Press.

USA4MilitaryFamilies.org, (2003). Active duty family members by state. Retrieved September 19, 2006, from http://usa4militaryfamilies.dod.mil

Urban Institute. (2006 April). *What about the dads? Child welfare agencies efforts to identify, locate, and involve nonresident fathers*. Washington,DC: Urban Institute.

U.S. Bureau of Justice Statistics. (2003). Crime Data Brief, Intimate Partner Violence, 1992-2001, in *The Facts on Domestic Violence*. San Francisco: Family Violence Prevention Fund. http://www.endabuse.org

U.S. Census Bureau. (2000). *America's Families and Living Arrangements* [Data file]. Available from Current Population Reports: http://www.census.gov/population/www/socdemo/hh-fam/p20-537_00.html

U.S. Census Bureau. (2005). *American factfinder detailed tables, B09001, B09003, & B09008, 2000* [Data file]. Available from American Community Survey: http://www.census.gov/acs/www/Products/index.htm

> **The Best Part of Being a Dad**
>
> "Watching and appreciating and interacting with another human being who is constantly evolving, developing and growing. Watching your kids grow into good young people while you have fun with them along the way."
>
> - from a father who completed the Father Involvement Survey, child's age 5-12 years

U.S. Census Bureau, (2005). Current population survey 2005. Retrieved March 15, 2006, from http://www.census.gov

U.S. Census Bureau. (2003). *Custodial Mothers and Fathers and Their Child Support: 2001* (Current Population Reports, P60-225). Washington, DC: Grall, T.

Bibliography and Acknowledgements

U.S. Census Bureau. (2003). *Married couple and unmarried-partner households:2000* (cnsr-5). Washington DC: Simmons, T. & O'Connell, M.

U.S. Census Bureau. (2004). *Stay at home parents top 5 million* [Data file]. Available from Census Bureau Reports: http://www.census.gov/Press-release/www/releases/archives/families_households/003118.html.

U.S. Census Bureau. (n.d.). *Technical note on same-sex unmarried partners.* Retrieved October 10, 2006, from http://www/census.gov/population/www/cen2000/samesex.html

U.S. Department of Education & U.S. Department of Health and Human Services. (2000). *A call to commitment: fathers' involvement in children's learning* (DOE Publication No. ED-99-PO-35580). Jessup, MD: Editorial Publications Center.

U.S. Department of Education, National Center for Education Statistics. *National Household EducationSurvey, 1999* [Computer file]. ICPSR version. Washington, DC: Department of Education.

Bibliography and Acknowledgements

Acknowledgements

Fatherhood Programs: Participants in Telephone Interview

During the spring of 2006, the following programs graciously supported the development of this publication by participating in a telephone interview. The results of the interviews have been included predominantly in the "Programs and Services" section.

American Credit & Equity Specialists
Audubon School ECFE
Bemidji Area Schools
Boyz II Dadz
Center for Integrated Well-Being Inc.
Central Center for Family Resources
Children's Home Society & Family Services
Cooperative Solutions Mediation Center
Council on Crime & Justice
Dads & Daughters
Dads' & Families Center
Dad's & Kids Activity Group
Dads & Kids, Barnes Early Childhood Center
Dads Make a Difference
Division of Indian Work
Edina Family Center
Elk River ECFE
Family Investment Center
FathersFIRST!
First Call for Help
Goodwill/Easter Seals FATHER Project
Grandkidsandme
Hermantown/Proctor Family Resource Center
Institute for Men's Health & Well-being
La Oportunidad Inc.
Lakes & Pines Community Action Council
Lao Family Community of Minnesota
Little Treasures Child Care & Family Center
Lutheran Social Service of Minnesota
Lutheran Social Service Positive Parenting
Parents as Teachers / Meld
Memorial Blood Centers
Men's Center
Minnesota Community Action Association
Minneapolis Public Schools
Minnesota Dads at Home
Minnesota Department of Health, Fathers' Adoption Registry
Northwest Youth & Family Services
Otter Tail - Wadena Community Action Council
Parents Are Important In Rochester
Parents Employment Program (PEP)
Park Rapids School District
PATH Inc.
Pillsbury United Communities
Pipestone/Jasper ECFE
Region VIII North Welfare Department
Resource Center for Fathers & Families
Reuben Lindh Learning Center
Rockford Area Schools
Southside Community Health Services
Southside Family Nurturing Center
St. Cloud ECFE
St. Mary's Medical Center
Tri-Valley ECFE
Tri-Valley Opportunity Council
Violence Intervention Project
Women's Health Center

Bibliography and Acknowledgements

Minnesota Fathers & Families Network: Board of Directors 2007

Rebecca Ahlstrand, Carlton County Child Support, Carlton

Jayne Anderson, Nicollet County Social Services, St. Peter

Mary Anderson, Fatherhood Advocate, Perham

Jason Giese, Southwest Minn. Private Industry Council, Montevideo

Jon Harper, Adventures in Fathering, Crystal

Jan Hayne, Dads Make a Difference, St. Paul

Michael Jerpbak, Crossroads College, Rochester

R. Clarence Jones, Southside Community Health Services, Minneapolis

Gar Kellom, St. John's Univ., Collegeville

Joe Kelly, Dads and Daughters, St. Paul

Joyce Lussier, Bemidji

Nancy Norbie, Kandiyohi County Family Services, Willmar

Glen Palm, St. Cloud State Univ., St. Cloud

Velura Peterson, Social Services, Virginia

Tamy Reese, Morris Early Childhood Family Education, Morris

Jack Sharp, Fatherhood Advocate, St. Cloud

Dwaine Simms, Twin Cities RISE!, Minneapolis

Enrique Soto, Banta Corporation, Long Prairie

Neil Tift, Dads and Families Center, Stillwater

Laura Turner, Employment / Fatherhood Advocate, St. Paul

Tina Welsh, Boyz II Dadz, Duluth

Planning Committee Members

Helen J. Bassett, Fathers' Adoption Registry, Minn. Dept. of Health

Diane Benjamin, Maternal and Child Health Training Program, Univ. of Minn. School of Public Health

Lee Buckley, Faith and Community Service Initiatives, Office of Governor Tim Pawlenty

Ellis F. Bullock, Grotto Foundation, Inc.

Wayland Campbell, Child Support Enforcement Division

Scott Chazdon, Transition Program Evaluation and Performance, Minn. Dept. of Human Services

Joan Danielson, Minn. Dept. of Employment & Econ. Development

Steve Erbes, Minn. Dept. of Employment & Econ. Development

Donald R. Eubanks, Minn. Dept. of Human Services

Andrew Freeberg, FATHER Project, Goodwill / Easter Seals

José González, Bush Foundation

Lowell Johnson

Robert Clarence Jones, Health Promotions Division, Southside Community Health Services

Tim Lanz, Offender Transition Services, Minnesota Department of Corrections

Bryan G. Nelson, MenTeach

Stephen L. Onell, FathersFIRST!

Dwaine R. Simms, Twin Cities RISE!

J. Neil Tift, Dads' and Families Center

Join the Minnesota Fathers & Families Network

Our Members: Anyone working on, or interested in, issues related to fathers and families in the state of Minnesota should consider joining the Minnesota Fathers & Families Network. As a professional development and networking organization, MFFN will help you to strengthen your work, learn from others around the state, and build the field of father and family services practitioners. Membership is open to the public.

Join us! Help improve the strength and sustainability of Minnesota's fatherhood programs.

Associate Member Benefits

Quarterly *Network Notes* Newsletter: A brief review of Network activities and father-related information.

Discounts to Conferences, Workshops, Publications: Special discounts to many Network activities and publications.

Get in the Loop: Join our email listserv of updates on legislative, budgetary, and policy developments, relevant research, funding opportunities and professional development opportunities.

Annual Members Meeting and Voting Privileges: Participation in meetings and policy information sessions, including the Annual Membership Meeting to share effective practices and inform MFFN priorities and agenda, the opportunity to serve on Network committees in your area of interest and participation in the election of the Network Board of Directors.

Nominate Award Recipients: MFFN members will nominate recipients for MFFN's annual awards.

Public Recognition: Members can demonstrate to funders and sponsors that they are actively engaged in Minnesota's fatherhood movement.

Leadership Circle Member Benefits

All Benefits of Associate Circle Members: Receive all of the benefits granted Associate Members.

Special Recognition: Recognized as leaders in the promotion of MFFN and fatherhood issues in Minnesota. Receive special recognition at select annual events and in select publications.

MFFN Membership Form

The Minnesota Fathers & Families Network offers a range of membership options to meet your needs. Membership must be renewed annually.

Select level:

- ☐ Individual "Associate Member": $20
- ☐ Individual "Leadership Circle Member": $50
- ☐ Organizational "Associate Member"*: $75
- ☐ Organizational "Leadership Circle Member"*: $200

Organizational Members may receive member benefits for no more than 5 individuals.

Please send check payable to "MFFN" to:
Minnesota Fathers & Families Network
161 Saint Anthony Ave. Suite 845 / Saint Paul, MN 55103

Member information:
Name, Job title: _____
Organization: _____
Address, City, State, Zip: _____
Email: _____
Phone: _____